A Journey into Biblical Stewardship

Stewardship as a Reflection of the Heart

ISBN: 9798340835017

Soft Cover

Independently published by Scott A Asselin, 2024

A Journey into Biblical Stewardship

First edition. September 2024

Copyright © 2024 Scott Asselin

Cover Design by April Sheffield, used with permission.

All Scripture quotations are taken from the King James Version.

All rights reserved. Neither this book, nor any parts within it may be sold or reproduced in any form without permission.

Then said Jesus unto his disciples, If any man will come after me, let him deny himself, and take up his cross, and follow me. (Matthew 16:24).

A question for Christians today - can we put Christ before all, deny ourselves, take up our cross, and follow Him with no effect on what we do with our money and possessions?

In a world filled with teachings about wealth that often overlook the Christian's call to stewardship, this book offers a deeper look into the relationship between our spiritual condition and our approach to money. Our attitudes and actions regarding possessions are not separate from our faith but are intimately tied to it. As Christ said, *"Ye cannot serve God and mammon" (Matthew 6:24).*

This book explores the profound impact that financial decisions have on our spiritual lives, the health of our families, and ultimately, our eternity. It's not about wealth-building strategies, but about dethroning the false gods of materialism to enthrone the one true God.

Here, you won't find formulas for net worth but questions that challenge how God measures your life. It's not about insurance, but assurance; not about securities, but security in Christ; not about trust funds, but trust in God. Through practical guidance anchored in Biblical principles, this book will lead you to view money and possessions through the lens of eternity, realizing that "Stewardship is a Reflection of the Heart".

Acknowledgments

I would like to express my deepest gratitude to all those who have taken the time to read, review, and proof *"A Journey into Biblical Stewardship"*. The insights, encouragement, and careful attention to detail provided have been invaluable in shaping this book, while contributing to making this journey more meaningful. Your input ensures that the message of stewardship is communicated clearly and thoughtfully. Your support is a true testament to the spirit of community and faith that this book seeks to promote. Thank you for walking alongside me in this endeavor. May God bless you abundantly for your time and effort.

I would be remiss in giving a special thanks to April Sheffield for the cover design art. Your hand drawn picture used on the cover is so greatly appreciated. Again, thank you so much.

A quick note from the author's desk

Since 1992 I have worked in the field of finance. During this time, I personally have seen the changes in how society views finance. While most financial principles taught by advisors today have a Biblical basis, they are presented from a self-serving basis. Recognizing this, we present this bible study with the purpose of focusing our attention back on God, who is the owner of all things. May this book serve as a beacon of light within the Christian world that has been darkened by greed, selfishness, and materialism.

Our prayer is that this book provides an illuminating light to a path of faithful stewardship, inspiring hearts to worship the One to whom all honor, praise, and glory belong by stirring us to honor God with every resource He has entrusted to our care. Recognizing the uniqueness of each individual's situation, we can each embrace the call to stewardship with humility, wisdom, and joy, as we seek to glorify God and advance His kingdom purposes on earth together.

A Journey into Biblical Stewardship

Table Of Contents

Ch 1	Embracing the Journey of Biblical Stewardship	1
Ch 2	God's Ownership and Our Stewardship	7
Ch 3	Walking in Integrity	13
Ch 4	Our Stewardship Responsibilities	19
Ch 5	The Faithfulness of Stewards	23
Ch 6	The Counter-Cultural Witness of Contentment	27
Ch 7	Cultivating Compassion in Stewardship	33
Ch 8	The Biblical Imperative of Generosity	39
Ch 9	A Godly Work Ethic	45
Ch 10	Sustainable Stewardship: A Biblical Perspective	51
Ch 11	Wise Planning	55
Ch 12	Debt Avoidance	63
Ch 13	Stewardship in an Eternal Perspective	71
Ch 14	Embracing the Call to Biblical Stewardship	77

A Journey into Biblical Stewardship

Embracing the Journey of Biblical Stewardship

In our world that is marked by relentless consumption, rampant materialism, and escalating environmental concerns, the pursuit of wealth, success, and comfort often consumes our thoughts and energies. This allows it to become easy to lose sight of the fundamental principles that lie at the heart of our existence. These principles are as ancient as the foundations of the earth, and as enduring as the heavens above. These are the timeless principles of Biblical stewardship which stand as a beacon of truth and hope. Rooted in the sacred pages of God's Word, these principles offer a holistic framework for managing resources with wisdom, integrity, and purpose. They remind us that stewardship is not merely a financial strategy or environmental ethic, rather it is a way of life, a sacred calling that encompasses every aspect of our existence. It is loudly proclaimed by David:

"The earth is the Lord's, and the fulness thereof; the world, and they that dwell therein." (Psalms 24:1)

In these simple yet profound words, we find the essence of Biblical stewardship, the recognition that everything we have, everything we are, and everything we aspire to be ultimately belongs to God. From the air we breathe to the ground we tread, from the talents we possess to the treasures we accumulate, all are gifts from the hand of our Creator, entrusted to us for a sacred purpose. At creation, God placed Adam and Eve as stewards over His creation. God then gave them instructions to oversee His creation.

"Be fruitful, and multiply, and replenish the earth, and subdue it: and have dominion over the fish of the sea, and over the fowl of the air, and over every living thing that moveth upon the earth."
(Genesis 1:28)

A Journey into Biblical Stewardship

In this divine commission, authority was granted to mankind to rule over the land, to wisely govern its resources, and to cultivate its abundance for the benefit of all – to be His stewards.

But what does it mean to be stewards of God's blessings? How do we navigate the complexities of life in a manner that honors the divine ownership of all things? These are the questions that lie at the heart of this book, a journey into the depths of Biblical stewardship, guided by the unfailing wisdom of Scripture.

Throughout the pages that follow, we will explore twelve principles of Biblical stewardship. These are foundational principles that illuminate the path of faithful stewardship and offer practical guidance for living a life with purpose and integrity, while being the framework of faithful stewardship that honors God and blesses others. Each principle is rooted in the Word of God, supported by the teachings of Jesus Christ and the insights of the Biblical writers. These principles, while not inclusive, are essential to lay a firm foundation that is rooted in the eternal truths of God's Word. From Genesis to Revelation, we encounter teachings that illuminate the path of faithful stewardship, forming the pillars upon which our understanding of Biblical stewardship is built. Twelve pillars, each one anchored in Scripture and bearing the weight of divine wisdom.

1. **Ownership Recognition** At the core of Biblical stewardship lies the recognition that everything belongs to God. As the psalmist declares,

    "The earth is the Lord's, and the fulness thereof; the world, and they that dwell therein." (Psalm 24:1)

    This foundational truth compels us to acknowledge God's sovereignty over all creation and embrace our role as stewards entrusted with managing His resources.

2. **Integrity** Integrity undergirds every aspect of Biblical stewardship, calling us to live in a manner that is honest, consistent, and true to God's Word. The Bible emphasizes that integrity is essential for a life that honors God and blesses others.

A Journey into Biblical Stewardship

> *"The integrity of the upright shall guide them: but the perverseness of transgressors shall destroy them." (Proverbs 11:3)*

Integrity involves more than just avoiding deceit; it is about aligning our actions with the truths of Scripture, being accountable for our decisions, and maintaining a pure heart before God and man.

3. **Accountability:** Alongside ownership recognition comes the principle of accountability. As stewards, we are called to manage God's resources with integrity and diligence, knowing that one day we will give an account for our stewardship. The apostle Paul reminds us:

> *"So then every one of us shall give account of himself to God." (Romans 14:12)*

4. **Faithfulness**: In the parable of the talents, Jesus commends faithful stewardship, declaring,

> *"Well done, thou good and faithful servant: thou hast been faithful over a few things, I will make thee ruler over many things: enter thou into the joy of thy lord." (Matthew 25:21)*

Faithfulness in stewardship involves using God-given resources wisely and productively for His kingdom purposes.

5. **Contentment**: In a culture marked by discontentment and consumerism, the Biblical principle of contentment stands as a counter-cultural witness. The apostle Paul writes:

> *"Not that I speak in respect of want: for I have learned, in whatsoever state I am, therewith to be content." (Philippians 4:11)*

A Journey into Biblical Stewardship

Contentment frees us from the endless pursuit of possessions and positions, enabling us to find true satisfaction in God alone.

6. **Compassion**: Central to Biblical stewardship is a heart of compassion and care for the marginalized and vulnerable. The wise king Solomon observes:

   "He that hath pity upon the poor lendeth unto the Lord; and that which he hath given will he pay him again." (Proverbs 19:17)

   Through acts of kindness and generosity, we demonstrate God's love to those in need, reflecting His heart of compassion.

7. **Generosity**: The Bible exhorts believers to embrace a spirit of generosity and giving. As Jesus teaches:

   "Give, and it shall be given unto you; good measure, pressed down, and shaken together, and running over, shall men give into your bosom. For with the same measure that ye mete withal it shall be measured to you again." (Luke 6:38)

   Generosity flows from a heart transformed by the grace of God, reflecting His lavish love and abundant provision.

8. **Work Ethic**: The Bible extols the virtues of diligence and hard work, affirming that:

   "Whatsoever thy hand findeth to do, do it with thy might." (Ecclesiastes 9:10)

   Work is a sacred calling, an opportunity to glorify God and serve others through the faithful stewardship of our time, talents, and energy.

A Journey into Biblical Stewardship

9. **Sustainability**: As stewards of God's creation, we are called to care for the earth and its resources responsibly. God's original mandate to humanity includes the charge to

   "replenish the earth, and subdue it." (Genesis 1:28)

   This stewardship extends to the environment, which has been entrusted to our care.

   "And the Lord God took the man, and put him into the garden of Eden to dress it and to keep it." (Genesis 2:15)

   Stewardship involves cultivating and preserving the earth's resources in a manner that honors God and promotes sustainability.

10. **Wise Planning**: Planning and foresight are integral components of faithful stewardship. The book of Proverbs affirms,

    "The thoughts of the diligent tend only to plenteousness; but of every one that is hasty only to want." (Proverbs 21:5)

    By seeking God's wisdom and guidance in our financial decisions, we can navigate life's uncertainties with confidence and clarity.

11. **Debt Avoidance**: The Scriptures caution against the dangers of Debt and the bondage it can bring. The wise sage Solomon advises,

    "The rich ruleth over the poor, and the borrower is servant to the lender." (Proverbs 22:7)

    By avoiding excessive debt and practicing financial prudence, we can experience greater freedom and flexibility in our stewardship.

A Journey into Biblical Stewardship

12. **Eternal Perspective**: Finally, Biblical stewardship is grounded in an eternal perspective that transcends the temporal pursuits of this world. The apostle Paul reminds us,

> *"For our conversation is in heaven; from whence also we look for the Saviour, the Lord Jesus Christ." (Philippians 3:20)*

By fixing our eyes on the eternal realities of God's kingdom, we gain perspective on the fleeting nature of earthly wealth and invest our resources in what truly matters for eternity.

It is our prayer that as we embark on this journey together, we do so with open hearts and eager minds, ready to discover the richness of God's provision and the beauty of His design for our lives. May we be transformed by the renewing of our minds, as we surrender our wills to His and embrace the call to stewardship with joy and gratitude. Note that as we delve into each pillar of Biblical stewardship, challenges and opportunities will be encountered, as well as trials and triumphs. There will be confrontation with our own limitations and weaknesses; at the same time, we will also discover the boundless grace and mercy of our Heavenly Father. Through it all, we will be reminded of the profound truth that underpins our journey that we are not owners but stewards, not masters but servants, entrusted with the privilege of managing God's resources for His glory and the flourishing of His creation.

A Journey into Biblical Stewardship

God's Ownership and Our Stewardship

Whether you are looking through the strongest telescope across the vast expanse of the cosmos or looking through a microscope to the tiniest part of an atom, everything in existence bears the mark of the Creator's handiwork. As the Psalmist proclaims:

"The earth is the Lord's, and the fulness thereof; the world, and they that dwell therein." (Psalm 24:1)

Found within this truth lies a foundational principle of our faith: the recognition that everything belongs to God. The universe, with its breathtaking beauty and intricate design, is His possession. Every mountain peak, every rolling wave, every whispering breeze declares His sovereignty.

"In the beginning, God created the heavens and the earth." (Genesis 1:1)

Not only the earth but the heavens, with their uncountable stars and galaxies, proclaim His glory.

"The heavens declare the glory of God; and the firmament sheweth his handywork." (Psalm 19:1)

In His wisdom and grace, God has entrusted us, His creation, with stewardship over His resources. We are not owners but stewards, called to manage God's possessions faithfully and wisely. Just as a steward oversees the affairs of his master's household, so are we tasked with the care and management of God's creation.

To grasp the full significance of this truth is to unlock the mystery of existence itself. It is to recognize that every particle of matter, every

A Journey into Biblical Stewardship

breath of life, every heartbeat resonates with the divine rhythm of creation. For in the beginning, when God spoke the universe into being, He established His sovereign claim over all that He had made. He is the Alpha and the Omega, the Beginning and the End, the Author and Sustainer of life.

As stewards of God's creation, we are called to embrace this foundational truth with humility and reverence. We are not proprietors but custodians, not masters but servants. Our tenure on this earth is but a fleeting moment in the grand tapestry of eternity. The wealth we accumulate, the possessions we cherish, the land we inhabit are all temporary gifts entrusted to us by the benevolence of our Creator.

In the Garden of Eden, God placed Adam and Eve as stewards over His creation. He blessed them and said to them,

"Be fruitful, and multiply, and replenish the earth, and subdue it: and have dominion over the fish of the sea, and over the fowl of the air, and over every living thing that moveth upon the earth."
(Genesis 1:28)

In this divine commission, humanity was granted authority to rule over the land, to govern its resources wisely, and to cultivate its abundance for the benefit of all. Yet we must be careful lest we mistake our stewardship for ownership. The earth and all its fullness belong to God alone.

We are but tenants in His vineyard, tenants entrusted with the care of His precious creation. As Jesus Himself taught in the parable of the talents,

"For the kingdom of heaven is as a man travelling into a far country, who called his own servants, and delivered unto them his goods." (Matthew 25:14)

Each servant received according to his ability, and each was held accountable for the use of his master's resources. Thus, we should approach our stewardship here with fear and trembling, with awe and wonder, with gratitude and humility. We need to recognize that every breath we draw, every morsel we eat, every possession we own is a gift from the hand of God.

We should use His resources wisely, for His glory and the betterment of His kingdom. In our stewardship, let us seek wisdom - the wisdom

A Journey into Biblical Stewardship

that comes from above, pure and peaceable, gentle and easy to be intreated.

"But the wisdom that is from above is first pure, then peaceable, gentle, and easy to be intreated, full of mercy and good fruits, without partiality, and without hypocrisy." (James 3:17)

Let us seek understanding - the understanding that God's ways are higher than our ways, and His thoughts than our thoughts.

"For as the heavens are higher than the earth, so are my ways higher than your ways, and my thoughts than your thoughts." (Isaiah 55:9)

Let us seek discernment - the discernment to distinguish between the fleeting treasures of this world and the enduring riches of heaven.

"Lay not up for yourselves treasures upon earth, where moth and rust doth corrupt, and where thieves break through and steal: But lay up for yourselves treasures in heaven, where neither moth nor rust doth corrupt, and where thieves do not break through nor steal: For where your treasure is, there will your heart be also." (Matthew 6:19-21)

As stewards of God's creation, we are called to be faithful and diligent in our responsibilities. We are called to cultivate the earth, to nurture its bounty, to protect its beauty, and to preserve its resources for future generations. We are called to be good stewards of our time, our talents, and our treasures, using them wisely and prudently for the advancement of God's kingdom.

Above all, let us remember that our stewardship is ultimately a matter of the heart. It is a reflection of our love for God as well as our love for our neighbor. It is a response to the grace and mercy that God has lavished upon us, even though we are but dust and ashes. It is a recognition that everything we have and everything we are belongs to Him who created us, sustains us, and redeems us.

"For of him, and through him, and to him, are all things: to whom be glory for ever. Amen." (Romans 11:36)

A Journey into Biblical Stewardship

Thus, our lives are to be a living testament to the truth that everything belongs to God. May we be found faithfully fulfilling our role as stewards entrusted with managing the precious resources God has bestowed upon us, whether it be our time, talents, finances, or the environment around us, with diligence and integrity.

As we are to use our resources for the glory of God and the advancement of His kingdom, our actions should reflect our recognition of God's ownership and our accountability to Him. We are reminded that one day, we will all stand before the judgment seat of Christ, to give an account of how we have stewarded the blessings entrusted to us.

> *"So then every one of us shall give account of himself to God."*
> *(Romans 14:12)*

Moreover, as our stewardship extends beyond mere material possessions, recognize that we are also stewards of the gospel, entrusted with the message of salvation and reconciliation through Jesus Christ.

> *"Let a man so account of us, as of the ministers of Christ, and stewards of the mysteries of God." (1 Corinthians 4:1)*

This precious gift is not to be hoarded but shared freely with others, that they too may come to know the saving grace of our Lord.

Despite our limited understanding and finite existence, God has chosen to entrust us with the management of His resources. This divine mandate confers upon humanity the responsibility to steward God's creation with wisdom, care, and diligence. As stewards entrusted with managing God's resources, we are called to exercise faithful stewardship in every aspect of our lives. This encompasses not only the material possessions we possess but also the time, talents, and opportunities entrusted to us by our Creator. Just as the master in Jesus' parable entrusted his servants with talents to invest and multiply, we also are called to use our gifts and resources wisely for the advancement of God's kingdom. *(read Matthew 25:14-30)*

Jesus imparts a profound lesson on stewardship through the parable of the unjust steward, highlighting the necessity of faithfulness and integrity in our management of what has been entrusted to us. This parable serves as a reminder that how we handle earthly possessions is

A Journey into Biblical Stewardship

a reflection of our dedication to God's kingdom. Notice what Jesus states:

"He that is faithful in that which is least is faithful also in much: and he that is unjust in the least is unjust also in much. If therefore ye have not been faithful in the unrighteous mammon, who will commit to your trust the true riches? And if ye have not been faithful in that which is another man's, who shall give you that which is your own?" (Luke 16:10-12)

We are reminded to recognize that all we possess is ultimately God's, and we are but stewards of His resources. Our faithfulness in managing even the smallest of these blessings reflects our readiness to be entrusted with the true riches of His kingdom.

A Journey into Biblical Stewardship

A Journey into Biblical Stewardship

Walking In Integrity

In the Christian life, integrity is not just an admirable trait but a cornerstone of spiritual maturity and effective stewardship. As stewards of God's creation, we are called to live lives of integrity, ensuring that our actions align with the principles of God's Word. Integrity encompasses honesty, ethical conduct, and unwavering adherence to moral principles, all of which are essential for a life that honors God.

The Bible is replete with references to integrity, highlighting its importance in the life of a believer.

> *"He that walketh uprightly walketh surely: but he that perverteth his ways shall be known." (Proverbs 10:9)*

This emphasizes that living with integrity provides a firm foundation, ensuring that we walk securely in our faith. On the other hand, a lack of integrity leads to a life of instability and exposure to the consequences of sin.

The book of Psalms also echoes the significance of integrity in the believer's life.

> *"Let integrity and uprightness preserve me; for I wait on thee." (Psalms 25:21)*

Here, the psalmist acknowledges that integrity and uprightness are not just moral choices but divine safeguards that preserve us in our walk with God. Integrity is not about perfection but about a sincere commitment to live according to God's standards, even when faced with challenges and temptations.

One of the most evident manifestations of integrity is honesty. As Christians, we are called to be honest in all our dealings, reflecting the truthfulness of God in our lives. Paul instructs us as follows:

A Journey into Biblical Stewardship

"Wherefore putting away lying, speak every man truth with his neighbor: for we are members one of another." (Ephesians 4:25)

Honesty is not optional for a believer; it is a requirement. Living a life of integrity means that we must be truthful in our words, transparent in our actions, and consistent in our character.

Integrity also involves open communication, especially when faced with difficult conversations. Jesus teaches us the importance of addressing conflicts directly:

"Moreover if thy brother shall trespass against thee, go and tell him his fault between thee and him alone: if he shall hear thee, thou hast gained thy brother." (Matthew 18:15)

This principle is not only applicable in resolving conflicts but also in maintaining integrity in our relationships. Rather than harboring resentment or avoiding uncomfortable situations, we must be willing to confront issues with honesty and love, reflecting the integrity of Christ in our interactions.

A life of integrity requires us to take responsibility for our actions, both good and bad. In a world that often encourages shifting blame or justifying wrongdoing, the Christian is called to a higher standard.

"He that covereth his sins shall not prosper: but whoso confesseth and forsaketh them shall have mercy." (Proverbs 28:13)

Admitting our mistakes and seeking forgiveness is an essential aspect of integrity. It is through this process that we grow spiritually and maintain a right relationship with God and others.

The story of King David provides a powerful example of integrity in the face of failure. After his sin with Bathsheba, David did not try to hide his transgression when confronted by the prophet Nathan. Instead, he confessed his sin and sought God's forgiveness, as recorded in Psalm 51. David's response demonstrates that integrity is not about being sinless but about being sincere in our repentance and committed to making things right.

Integrity is also about respecting boundaries, both our own and those of others.

A Journey into Biblical Stewardship

"Be kindly affectioned one to another with brotherly love; in honor preferring one another." (Romans 12:10)

This highlights the importance of respecting others, not just in our actions but in our thoughts and attitudes as well. Whether it's in our personal relationships or within our community, integrity demands that we honor the boundaries that protect the dignity and well-being of others.

For example, respecting someone's privacy, time, and values is a reflection of integrity. It means not prying into matters that are not our concern, not overstepping our roles, and being mindful of the impact our actions have on others. By respecting these boundaries, we not only uphold our integrity but also demonstrate the love and consideration that God calls us to exhibit in our relationships.

A life of integrity is marked by a genuine desire to help others. Notice what the apostle Paul says:

"Bear ye one another's burdens, and so fulfill the law of Christ." (Galatians 6:2)

This underscores the importance of compassion and service in the Christian life. However, integrity also requires us to balance our desire to help with the necessity of self-care. Jesus Himself modeled this balance, often withdrawing to pray and rest, even as He ministered to the needs of others.

"And in the morning, rising up a great while before day, he went out, and departed into a solitary place, and there prayed." (Mark 1:35)

Helping others should not come at the expense of our own health and well-being. True integrity involves recognizing our limitations and ensuring that we are spiritually, emotionally, and physically equipped to serve effectively. By taking care of ourselves, we are better able to fulfill our God-given responsibilities and continue to serve others in a sustainable way.

Integrity also involves being reliable and trustworthy. Jesus teaches us this when he says:

A Journey into Biblical Stewardship

"But let your communication be, Yea, yea; Nay, nay: for whatsoever is more than these cometh of evil." (Matthew 5:37)

This emphasizes the importance of keeping our word and being dependable in all that we do. Whether it's in fulfilling a promise or completing a task, integrity means that others can trust us to follow through on our commitments.

Reliability is not just about what we do but how we do it. Notice Paul's instructions:

"And whatsoever ye do, do it heartily, as to the Lord, and not unto men; Knowing that of the Lord ye shall receive the reward of the inheritance: for ye serve the Lord Christ." (Colossians 3:23-24)

When we approach our responsibilities with this mindset, we demonstrate integrity by working diligently and faithfully, knowing that our ultimate accountability is to God.

Life is full of unexpected challenges, and how we respond to them is a true test of our integrity.

"My brethren, count it all joy when ye fall into divers temptations; Knowing this, that the trying of your faith worketh patience. But let patience have her perfect work, that ye may be perfect and entire, wanting nothing." (James 1:2-4)

Integrity involves responding to life's difficulties with patience and flexibility, trusting that God is working through every situation to refine our character.

A person of integrity does not give up easily, nor become disheartened when things do not go as planned. Instead, they remain steadfast in their faith, trusting in God's sovereignty and goodness. This resilience is not born out of mere stubbornness but out of a deep conviction that God is in control and that His plans are ultimately for our good.

"And we know that all things work together for good to them that love God, to them who are the called according to his purpose." (Romans 8:28)

A Journey into Biblical Stewardship

Integrity is essential in our role as stewards of God's resources. Notice what Jesus says on this.

"He that is faithful in that which is least is faithful also in much: and he that is unjust in the least is unjust also in much."
(Luke 16:10)

This principle applies to all areas of life, from how we manage our finances to how we use our time and talents. As stewards, we are called to be faithful in even the smallest tasks, knowing that our integrity in these areas reflects our trustworthiness in larger matters.

For instance, being diligent in managing our finances with integrity means being honest in our transactions, avoiding debt, and using our resources to bless others. It also means being transparent and accountable in our financial dealings, ensuring that our actions align with Biblical principles. When we handle our resources with integrity, we demonstrate our faithfulness to God and our commitment to using what He has entrusted to us for His glory.

Living a life of integrity brings many rewards, both in this life and in the life to come.

"The integrity of the upright shall guide them: but the perverseness of transgressors shall destroy them." (Proverbs 11:3)

Integrity serves as a guiding principle, leading us in the paths of righteousness and protecting us from the pitfalls of sin. Moreover, integrity brings peace and confidence, knowing that we are living in alignment with God's will.

In addition to the spiritual benefits, integrity also has practical rewards. A person of integrity earns the trust and respect of others, builds strong relationships, and experiences a sense of fulfillment that comes from living a life of purpose. Ultimately, the greatest reward of integrity is the assurance of God's pleasure and the promise of eternal life with Him.

"His lord said unto him, Well done, thou good and faithful servant: thou hast been faithful over a few things, I will make thee ruler over many things: enter thou into the joy of thy lord." (Matthew 25:21)

A Journey into Biblical Stewardship

Integrity is not just a characteristic of a Christian; it is the essence of what it means to be a follower of Christ. As we strive to live lives of integrity, we must remember that our actions reflect the character of the God we serve. In every area of our lives, whether in our relationships, our stewardship, or our response to challenges, let us commit to walking in integrity, trusting that God will guide and bless us as we seek to honor Him. May we, like the psalmist, pray:

"Let integrity and uprightness preserve me; for I wait on thee,"
(Psalm 25:21)

and may our lives be a testimony to the power of God's grace working through us as we live out our call to Biblical stewardship.

A Journey into Biblical Stewardship

Our Stewardship Responsibilities

With the recognition of God's ownership lies the principle of accountability. This principle is a sobering reminder that as stewards, we are called to manage God's resources with integrity and diligence, knowing that one day we will give an account for our stewardship. The apostle Paul, in his letter to the Romans, articulates this truth with clarity and conviction:

"So then every one of us shall give account of himself to God." (Romans 14:12)

These words serve as a clarion call to accountability, echoing down through the corridors of time and piercing the depths of the human soul.

But what does it mean to be accountable as stewards of God's resources? It means recognizing that our actions have consequences, not just in the temporal realm, but in the eternal realm as well. It means acknowledging that every decision we make, every resource we steward, and every opportunity we seize carries weight and significance in the eyes of God. Consider our position as stewards. The Psalmist declares,

"Thou madest him to have dominion over the works of thy hands; thou hast put all things under his feet" (Psalm 8:6).

We are reminded of the authority bestowed upon humanity by the Creator Himself. God, in His infinite wisdom, has entrusted us with dominion over the earth and all its inhabitants. Our position is one of stewardship: a sacred trust to manage His creation in accordance with His will.

The apostle Paul underscores our role as stewards when he writes,

A Journey into Biblical Stewardship

"For if I do this thing willingly, I have a reward: but if against my will, a dispensation of the gospel is committed unto me,"
(1 Corinthians 9:17)

Paul acknowledges that the gospel ministry entrusted to him is not his own but a divine commission. In like manner our stewardship of God's resources is not a matter of personal entitlement, but a responsibility given to us by God.

We must then ask what the responsibilities of a steward are. As stated, this begins with recognizing God as Owner. True discipleship requires a radical commitment to prioritize God above all else. Jesus teaches,

"So likewise, whosoever he be of you that forsaketh not all that he hath, he cannot be my disciple." (Luke 14:33)

This includes recognizing God as the rightful owner of all things and surrendering our lives and possessions to His lordship.

It then follows that we must be faithful. The apostle Paul affirms this in his communications to the believers in Corinth.

"Moreover it is required in stewards, that a man be found faithful."
(1 Corinthians 4:2)

Faithfulness is the hallmark of effective stewardship. It involves loyalty, reliability, and steadfastness in carrying out the responsibilities entrusted to us by God.

This then leads to us being obedient and seeking the Lord. Moses gave specific instructions to the Israelites on this matter.

"Save when there shall be no poor among you; for the Lord shall greatly bless thee in the land which the Lord thy God giveth thee for an inheritance to possess it." (Deuteronomy 15:4-5)

Obedience to God's commands and seeking His guidance are essential aspects of faithful stewardship. When we align our actions with His will, we experience His abundant blessings.

This then brings us to trusting in the Lord. The book of Proverbs addresses this as Solomon reminds us,

A Journey into Biblical Stewardship

"By humility and the fear of the Lord are riches, and honour, and life." (Proverbs 22:4)

Trusting in the Lord rather than in ourselves or our possessions is fundamental to wise stewardship. It requires humility, recognizing our dependence on God for provision and guidance.

With these responsibilities comes a level of accountability for our stewardship. Jesus tells a parable about a steward who was called to give an account of his management.

"And he called him, and said unto him, How is it that I hear this of thee? give an account of thy stewardship; for thou mayest be no longer steward." (Luke 16:2)

Similarly, the apostle Paul writes,

"For we must all appear before the judgment seat of Christ; that every one may receive the things done in his body, according to that he hath done, whether it be good or bad." (2 Corinthians 5:10)

We find in the book of Revelation that John sees a vision of the final judgment and records the following:

"the dead were judged out of those things which were written in the books, according to their works." (Revelation 20:12)

These passages underscore the reality of our accountability before God. As stewards, we are entrusted with the care of His resources, and we will be held to account for how we have managed them. Of great concern is the fact that this accountability extends beyond this earthly life into the realms of eternity, where every thought, word, and deed will be scrutinized in the light of God's righteous judgment.

As stewards entrusted with the care of God's creation, we are called to embrace our responsibilities with humility, faithfulness, and obedience.

"Moreover it is required in stewards, that a man be found faithful." (1 Corinthians 4:2)

Recognizing the Lord as the true owner of all, we must be diligent in our stewardship, seeking His guidance in all our endeavors.

A Journey into Biblical Stewardship

"Trust in the LORD with all thine heart; and lean not unto thine own understanding. In all thy ways acknowledge Him, and He shall direct thy paths." (Proverbs 3:5-6)

Let us also live each day with the understanding that we shall give an account of our stewardship before the judgment seat of Christ.

"So then every one of us shall give account of himself to God." (Romans 14:12)

May we strive to be faithful stewards, longing to hear the words of our Master:

"Well done, thou good and faithful servant." (Matthew 25:21)

A Journey into Biblical Stewardship

Chapter Five

The Faithfulness of Stewards

As we continue our journey towards Biblical Stewardship, a melody can be heard that resounds with unwavering clarity. It is called faithfulness, and it is echoing the heartbeat of our commitment to God. As stewards entrusted with the treasures of heaven, our commitment is not a mere obligation but a sacred calling that is woven into the fabric of our identity as disciples of Christ. As stewards entrusted with the treasures of our Master, our fidelity is paramount, reflecting the very character of the One whom we serve.

Looking at the words of Christ we find a profound illustration of faithful stewardship.

"His lord said unto him, Well done, thou good and faithful servant: thou hast been faithful over a few things, I will make thee ruler over many things: enter thou into the joy of thy lord." (Matthew 25:21)

The faithful steward, entrusted with the talents of his master, invested in them wisely and reaped a bountiful harvest of commendation and reward. Faithfulness is not merely a commendable trait but an essential requirement for those who have been entrusted with the treasures of the Kingdom.

Faithfulness is a steadfast commitment to honor God with our time, talents, and treasures, regardless of the circumstances that may surround us. Our call from God is to live a life that consist of trusting God moment-by-moment with obedience no matter the circumstance that is ordained for us. It's not our wealth or poverty, fame or obscurity, level of fulfillment or boredom, nor our power or helplessness. Like Hezekiah, how we faithfully know and do the Word of God will be the measure of our success.

A Journey into Biblical Stewardship

"And thus did Hezekiah throughout all Judah, and wrought that which was good and right and truth before the LORD his God. And in every work that he began in the service of the house of God, and in the law, and in the commandments, to seek his God, he did it with all his heart, and prospered." (II Chronicles 31:20-21)

As stewards entrusted with the riches of our Master, we must explore the profound significance of faithfulness and its transformative power in our stewardship journey in each and every area of our lives. Consider the following:

- Time is a precious commodity entrusted to our care. It has been referred to as the currency of life. How we invest our time reflects our priorities and values. The psalmist implores us:

    "So teach us to number our days, that we may apply our hearts unto wisdom." (Psalm 90:12)

    Faithfulness in stewardship demands that we redeem the time, using each moment wisely for the glory of God.

    "See then that ye walk circumspectly, not as fools, but as wise, Redeeming the time, because the days are evil." (Ephesians 5:15-16)

- Every individual possesses a unique array of gifts and abilities bestowed by the hand of our Creator. Whether it be the gift of teaching, hospitality, or craftsmanship, each talent is a precious resource to be cultivated and utilized for the advancement of God's Kingdom. Jesus illustrates the principle of faithful stewardship in the parable of the talents found in **Matthew 25:14-30**. Notice how Jesus commends those who invested their talents wisely:

    "His lord said unto him, Well done, thou good and faithful servant: thou hast been faithful over a few things, I will make thee ruler over many things: enter thou into the joy of thy lord." (Matthew 25:21)

A Journey into Biblical Stewardship

and then Jesus reproves the one who buried his talent out of fear.

> *"His lord answered and said unto him, Thou wicked and slothful servant, thou knewest that I reap where I sowed not, and gather where I have not strawed: Thou oughtest therefore to have put my money to the exchangers, and then at my coming I should have received mine own with usury. Take therefore the talent from him, and give it unto him which hath ten talents. For unto every one that hath shall be given, and he shall have abundance: but from him that hath not shall be taken away even that which he hath. And cast ye the unprofitable servant into outer darkness: there shall be weeping and gnashing of teeth."*
> *(Matthew 25:26-30)*

- Material possessions, though fleeting, wield significant influence over our lives. Our stewardship of wealth and possessions serves as a litmus test of our faithfulness to God. Jesus admonishes,

> *"Lay not up for yourselves treasures upon earth, where moth and rust doth corrupt, and where thieves break through and steal: But lay up for yourselves treasures in heaven."*
> *(Matthew 6:19-20)*

Faithfulness in stewardship requires that we use our resources wisely, generously sharing with those in need and investing in eternal treasures.

An observation should be made here that the crucible of adversity is the forge in which the steel of faithfulness is tempered. Joseph, sold into slavery by his own brothers, remained faithful to his God and his master, ultimately rising to prominence as the steward of Egypt.

> *"And Joseph found grace in his sight, and he served him: and he made him overseer over his house, and all that he had he put into his hand." (Genesis 39:4)*

A Journey into Biblical Stewardship

Despite the trials and tribulations that beset him, Joseph clung steadfastly to the promises of God, knowing that His faithfulness endures forever.

"Thy faithfulness is unto all generations: thou hast established the earth, and it abideth." (Psalm 119:90)

Faithfulness is not merely a fleeting emotion or a passing fancy, but rather it is a steadfast commitment to the task at hand, regardless of the circumstances. Notice the prophet Samuel, from his youth until old age, served the Lord with unwavering devotion.

"And now, behold, the king walketh before you: and I am old and grayheaded; and, behold, my sons are with you: and I have walked before you from my childhood unto this day." (1 Samuel 12:2)

Whether in times of prosperity or scarcity, Samuel remained faithful in his charge, fulfilling his responsibilities with diligence and integrity.

We see the apostle Paul exhorts his fellow laborers,

"Moreover it is required in stewards, that a man be found faithful." (1 Corinthians 4:2)

Whether in seasons of abundance or scarcity, in times of joy or sorrow, the faithful steward remains steadfast in his service, unwavering in his devotion to his Master.

As we journey along the path of stewardship, our faithfulness does not go unnoticed by the One who holds the universe in His hands.

"Blessed is that servant, whom his lord when he cometh shall find so doing." (Matthew 24:46)

The faithful steward is the one who diligently tends to the affairs of his Master, realizing they do not have the right to pick and choose. If we are faithful in all matters, including the least important thing, and those things we do not like, then we will one day hear the words of commendation and receive the reward of his faithfulness.

A Journey into Biblical Stewardship

The Counter-Cultural Witness of Contentment

Within the framework of Biblical stewardship, contentment emerges as a guiding principle throughout the journey. It helps us gain a deeper understanding of God's provision and our role as faithful stewards. In a world consumed by consumerism and driven by the insatiable desire for more, this Biblical principle of contentment stands as a counter-cultural witness. It is a beacon of light amidst the darkness of discontentment and materialism. Rooted in the timeless truths of Scripture, contentment offers a pathway to freedom from the relentless pursuit of possessions and positions, leading us to discover true satisfaction in God alone.

"Not that I speak in respect of want: for I have learned, in whatsoever state I am, therewith to be content," (Philippians 4:11)

Paul, speaking these timeless words, shines a beacon of truth, illuminating the path to true satisfaction and fulfillment in God.

From the very outset of our stewardship journey, God extends a gracious invitation to partake of His goodness and find contentment in Him alone.

"O taste and see that the Lord is good: blessed is the man that trusteth in him." (Psalm 34:8)

This invitation beckons us to immerse ourselves in the richness of God's presence, discovering that true contentment is found in knowing and trusting Him. Contentment, therefore, is not merely a fleeting emotion tied to our circumstances but a steadfast conviction that transcends the highs and lows of life. It frees us from the shackles of covetousness and greed, enabling us to find fulfillment and peace in every season, whether in abundance or in lack.

A Journey into Biblical Stewardship

Similarly, Peter encourages us to desire the pure milk of the Word, which nourishes our souls and leads to spiritual growth and contentment.

"As newborn babes, desire the sincere milk of the word, that ye may grow thereby: If so be ye have tasted that the Lord is gracious."
(1 Peter 2:2-3)

As stewards, we are called to partake of God's Word daily, allowing His truth to shape our hearts and minds and anchor our contentment in Him.

Contentment is not merely a passive state, but rather it is first a learned trait that is cultivated through our relationship with the Lord; and secondly a choice to trust God. Paul affirms this truth when he proclaims:

"I know both how to be abased, and I know how to abound: everywhere and in all things I am instructed both to be full and to be hungry, both to abound and to suffer need." (Philipians. 4:12)

Through his own experiences, Paul learned the secret of contentment. It was not through external circumstances but through his unwavering trust in God's faithfulness and provision. Similarly, partaking in the goodness of God matures our appetite to be more like Christ. John records Jesus saying,

" But he said unto them, I have meat to eat that ye know not of. Therefore said the disciples one to another, Hath any man brought him ought to eat? Jesus saith unto them, My meat is to do the will of him that sent me, and to finish his work." (John 4:32-34)

As we partake of God's Word and align our desires with His will, our appetite for worldly things diminishes, and we find true contentment in fulfilling God's purposes for our lives.

Contentment springs forth from a desire for Christ above all else. As the Psalmist declares:

"Whom have I in heaven but thee? and there is none upon earth that I desire beside thee." (Psalms 73:25)

A Journey into Biblical Stewardship

When Christ becomes the center of our lives, our pursuit of worldly possessions and pleasures fades in comparison to the surpassing worth of knowing Him. However, our human nature often leads us to chase after the fleeting treasures of this world.

"He that loveth silver shall not be satisfied with silver; nor he that loveth abundance with increase: this is also vanity."
(Ecclesiastes 5:10-12)

The quest for wealth and worldly success ultimately leads to disillusionment and emptiness, for true satisfaction cannot be found in material possessions alone.

Contentment blossoms when we cultivate a grateful heart and learn to appreciate the blessings that surround us each day. As stewards entrusted with God's resources, we are called to embrace the principle of contentment wholeheartedly. For this reason, in the midst of life's complexities, finding joy in simple things becomes paramount to cultivating contentment.

"There is nothing better for a man, than that he should eat and drink, and that he should make his soul enjoy good in his labour. This also I saw, that it was from the hand of God."
(Ecclesiastes 2:24-26)

When we learn to find joy in the everyday blessings that God provides, we discover a contentment that transcends circumstances. Thus, we find that contentment is not contingent upon our external circumstances but is rooted in our relationship with Christ, who empowers us to find joy and satisfaction in Him alone.

Thus, we find the Scripture exhorts us to be content, not anxious about our lives and needs. Jesus reiterates this to us.

"Therefore I say unto you, Take no thought for your life, what ye shall eat, or what ye shall drink; nor yet for your body, what ye shall put on." (Matthew 6:25)

Similarly, we find Paul reminding us of the same thing.

A Journey into Biblical Stewardship

"Let your conversation be without covetousness; and be content with such things as ye have: for he hath said, I will never leave thee, nor forsake thee." (Hebrews 13:5)

Paul writes to Timothy about being content with our basic needs.

"And having food and raiment let us be therewith content." (1 Timothy 6:8)

Notice that Jesus instructs the soldiers with this same thought.

"And the soldiers likewise demanded of him, saying, And what shall we do? And he said unto them, Do violence to no man, neither accuse any falsely; and be content with your wages." (Luke 3:14)

As stewards entrusted with God's resources, we are called to cultivate contentment in every aspect of our lives. Paul reinforces this thought when he writes:

" But I rejoiced in the Lord greatly, that now at the last your care of me hath flourished again; wherein ye were also careful, but ye lacked opportunity. Not that I speak in respect of want: for I have learned, in whatsoever state I am, therewith to be content. I know both how to be abased, and I know how to abound: every where and in all things I am instructed both to be full and to be hungry, both to abound and to suffer need. I can do all things through Christ which strengtheneth me." (Philippians 4:10-13)

Whether in times of abundance or scarcity, our contentment is anchored in our relationship with God and His faithfulness to provide for our needs. Ultimately, contentment, when it is coupled with godliness, will bring great gain.

"But godliness with contentment is great gain." (1 Timothy 6:6)

As we journey through the landscape of Biblical stewardship, we see that the Biblical principle of contentment stands as a timeless truth that transcends cultural trends and societal norms. It is a transformative mindset that leads to freedom from the bondage of materialism and a deeper intimacy with God. As we cultivate contentment in our lives,

A Journey into Biblical Stewardship

may we experience the richness of God's provision and the abundance of His grace, finding true satisfaction in Him alone.

A Journey into Biblical Stewardship

A Journey into Biblical Stewardship

Chapter Seven

Cultivating Compassion in Stewardship

In our journey to Biblical stewardship, compassion plays a pivotal role. Compassionate stewardship goes beyond mere management of resources; it reflects a deep commitment to loving and serving others as Christ did. The Bible is replete with examples and exhortations to act with compassion, emphasizing its importance in our daily lives and our stewardship responsibilities. There exists the Biblical foundation for compassionate stewardship, illustrating how we can integrate compassion into our management of God's resources.

Compassion is a fundamental attribute of God's character and a central theme in the teachings of Jesus. As stewards, we are called to reflect God's compassion in our interactions and management of resources. The Bible repeatedly affirms God's compassionate nature.

"The Lord is merciful and gracious, slow to anger, and plenteous in mercy." (Psalm 103:8)

This verse highlights God's abundant mercy and patience, setting a standard for us to emulate.

"It is of the Lord's mercies that we are not consumed, because his compassions fail not. They are new every morning: great is thy faithfulness." (Lamentations 3:22-23)

God's unwavering compassion and faithfulness provide a model for our own behavior as stewards.

Jesus Christ, the ultimate steward, exemplified compassion throughout His ministry.

A Journey into Biblical Stewardship

"But when he saw the multitudes, he was moved with compassion on them, because they fainted, and were scattered abroad, as sheep having no shepherd." (Matthew 9:36)

Jesus' compassion led Him to teach, heal, and provide for those in need. His life demonstrates that true stewardship involves caring deeply for others and addressing their needs.

The New Testament encourages believers to adopt a lifestyle of compassion. Paul gives us instruction concerning this.

"Put on therefore, as the elect of God, holy and beloved, bowels of mercies, kindness, humbleness of mind, meekness, longsuffering." (Colossians 3:12)

This verse underscores the importance of embodying merciful and kind attitudes, which are essential for compassionate stewardship.

"Finally, be ye all of one mind, having compassion one of another, love as brethren, be pitiful, be courteous." (1 Peter 3:8)

Compassion is thus not optional but a mandate for those who follow Christ.

To integrate compassion into our stewardship, we must adhere to certain principles that guide our actions and decisions.

1. **Recognize the Needs Around You** - Compassionate stewards are attentive to the needs of others.

   "The righteous considereth the cause of the poor: but the wicked regardeth not to know it." (Proverbs 29:7)

   Recognizing the needs around us requires sensitivity and awareness. We must actively seek to understand the challenges faced by those in our communities and beyond.

2. **Respond Generously** - Generosity is a natural outflow of compassion.

A Journey into Biblical Stewardship

"He that hath pity upon the poor lendeth unto the Lord; and that which he hath given will he pay him again."
(Proverbs 19:17)

When we give generously to those in need, we honor God and reflect His character. Our resources, whether financial, material, or time, should be used to alleviate the suffering of others.

3. **Serve with Humility** - Humility is essential for compassionate stewardship.

   "Let nothing be done through strife or vainglory; but in lowliness of mind let each esteem other better than themselves. Look not every man on his own things, but every man also on the things of others." (Philippians 2:3-4)

   Serving with humility means prioritizing the well-being of others above our own interests, recognizing that our role as stewards is to serve, not to be served.

4. **Foster Relationships** - Building and nurturing relationships is a key aspect of compassionate stewardship. Jesus emphasized relational ministry, investing time in individuals and communities.

   "A new commandment I give unto you, That ye love one another; as I have loved you, that ye also love one another. By this shall all men know that ye are my disciples, if ye have love one to another." (John 13:34-35)

   Genuine relationships allow us to understand and meet the deeper needs of those we serve.

5. **Advocate for Justice** - Compassionate stewards also advocate for justice and fairness as established by God's requirements.

   "He hath shewed thee, O man, what is good; and what doth the Lord require of thee, but to do justly, and to love mercy, and to walk humbly with thy God?" (Micah 6:8)

A Journey into Biblical Stewardship

Advocacy involves speaking out against injustice and working towards equitable solutions for those who are marginalized or oppressed.

Applying these principles involves tangible actions that demonstrate our commitment to compassionate stewardship. Here are several ways we can practice compassion in our stewardship.

1. **Providing for the Poor** - One of the most direct ways to exercise compassionate stewardship is by providing for the poor.

   "He that hath a bountiful eye shall be blessed; for he giveth of his bread to the poor." (Proverbs 22:9)

   Whether through personal donations, supporting charitable organizations, or engaging in community outreach, our resources can make a significant difference in the lives of those who are less fortunate.

2. **Caring for the Sick** - Caring for the sick is another vital aspect of compassionate stewardship. Notice that Jesus identifies Himself with the needy:

   "Naked, and ye clothed me: I was sick, and ye visited me: I was in prison, and ye came unto me." (Matthew 25:36)

   Visiting the sick, providing medical support, or simply offering comfort and companionship are ways we can fulfill this calling.

3. **Supporting the Bereaved** - Supporting those who are grieving is a profound expression of compassion.

   "Rejoice with them that do rejoice, and weep with them that weep." (Romans 12:15)

   Being present for those who are mourning, offering emotional support, and helping with practical needs are important aspects of compassionate stewardship.

A Journey into Biblical Stewardship

4. **Mentoring and Discipleship** - Mentoring and discipling others is a form of compassionate stewardship that invests in people's spiritual and personal growth.

   "And the things that thou hast heard of me among many witnesses, the same commit thou to faithful men, who shall be able to teach others also." (2 Timothy 2:2)

   By mentoring others, we help them develop their God-given potential and prepare them to be effective stewards themselves.

5. **Practicing Hospitality** - Hospitality is a practical expression of compassion.

   "Be not forgetful to entertain strangers: for thereby some have entertained angels unawares." (Hebrews 13:2)

   Welcoming others into our homes and lives, providing meals, and creating a warm, inclusive environment are ways we can practice hospitality.

Compassionate stewardship has a profound impact, both on the individuals we serve and on our own spiritual growth. It begins by transforming lives which leads to fostering a sense of community. This leads to personal growth and blessing, while being a powerful witness to the world. Consider the impact of each of these areas.

Compassionate stewardship transforms lives by meeting physical, emotional, and spiritual needs. When we act with compassion, we become instruments of God's love and mercy, bringing hope and healing to those who are suffering. Jesus encourages this:

"Let your light so shine before men, that they may see your good works, and glorify your Father which is in heaven." (Matthew 5:16)

Our compassionate actions can lead others to glorify God and experience His love.

Compassionate stewardship fosters a sense of community and belonging. We find this describes the early church's communal lifestyle:

A Journey into Biblical Stewardship

"And all that believed were together, and had all things common; And sold their possessions and goods, and parted them to all men, as every man had need." (Acts 2:44-45)

By sharing resources and supporting one another, we build strong, supportive communities that reflect the kingdom of God.

Practicing compassionate stewardship also contributes to our own personal growth.

"The liberal soul shall be made fat: and he that watereth shall be watered also himself." (Proverbs 11:25)

As we give of ourselves, we experience spiritual enrichment and growth. Compassionate actions deepen our faith, enhance our empathy, and draw us closer to God.

Finally, our compassionate stewardship serves as a powerful witness to the world.

"By this shall all men know that ye are my disciples, if ye have love one to another." (John 13:35)

When we act with compassion, we demonstrate the reality of God's love and attract others to the faith. Our stewardship becomes a living testimony of the transformative power of Christ's love.

Compassion is at the heart of Biblical stewardship. By recognizing the needs around us, responding generously, serving with humility, fostering relationships, and advocating for justice, we can practice compassionate stewardship that honors God and serves others. The impact of such stewardship is transformative, touching lives, building communities, and witnessing to the world. As we journey toward Biblical stewardship, let us commit to reflecting God's compassion in all that we do, embodying the love of Christ through our stewardship. In doing so, we fulfill our calling as faithful stewards, bringing glory to God and hope to those we serve.

A Journey into Biblical Stewardship

The Biblical Imperative of Generosity

Along this journey to Biblical stewardship we see a vibrant color intricately woven into the fabric of our faith, which is generosity. From the beginning of time, God's Word exhorts believers to embrace a spirit of generosity and giving, mirroring the very heart of our Creator. Jesus, in His timeless teachings, imparts to us this particular profound truth.

"Give, and it shall be given unto you; good measure, pressed down, and shaken together, and running over, shall men give into your bosom. For with the same measure that ye mete withal it shall be measured to you again." (Luke 6:38)

The principle of reciprocity is laid bare, which simply stated means the more generously we give, the more abundantly we receive. This is not merely in material blessings, but rather in the overflow of God's grace and provision in our lives.

Generosity, however, is not merely a transactional act, rather it is the reflection of the transformative power of God's grace. Generosity flows from the heart that has been touched and transformed by the boundless love and abundant provision of our Heavenly Father. Being the recipients of His lavish grace, we become the conduits of His generosity, extending His love and provision to those around us.

Yet it should be noted that our generosity will face tests. These tests that reveal the authenticity of our faith, the depth of God's love within us, and our commitment to living as faithful stewards of His blessings. The acid test of giving is articulated in James.

"Even so faith, if it hath not works, is dead, being alone." (James 2:17)

A Journey into Biblical Stewardship

Notice that James points out that our generosity must be more than mere words or intentions; it must be accompanied by tangible actions that reflect our faith and love in action.

Furthermore, the test of God's love abiding in us is intimately tied to our willingness to give sacrificially. We are admonished by John:

> *"But whoso hath this world's good, and seeth his brother have need, and shutteth up his bowels of compassion from him, how dwelleth the love of God in him?" (1 John 3:17)*

We see from this that the measure of God's love within us is evidenced by our compassion and generosity towards those in need. This is why loving our neighbor, as exemplified in the parable of the Good Samaritan, is another crucial aspect of demonstrating generosity.

> *"But a certain Samaritan, as he journeyed, came where he was: and when he saw him, he had compassion on him, And went to him, and bound up his wounds, pouring in oil and wine, and set him on his own beast, and brought him to an inn, and took care of him. And on the morrow when he departed, he took out two pence, and gave them to the host, and said unto him, Take care of him; and whatsoever thou spendest more, when I come again, I will repay thee." (Luke 10:33-35)*

It challenges us to transcend barriers and prejudices, extending a helping hand to anyone in need, regardless of their social status, background, or circumstances.

Moreover, we find the test of lordship confronts us with the question of where our ultimate allegiance lies. Jesus instructs the rich young ruler:

> *"If thou wilt be perfect, go and sell that thou hast, and give to the poor, and thou shalt have treasure in heaven: and come and follow me." (Matthew 19:21)*

Notice that this reveals generosity as being a litmus test of our willingness to surrender all to Christ. In doing so, our actions display acknowledging His lordship over every aspect of our lives, including our possessions.

A Journey into Biblical Stewardship

Understanding God's attitude in giving is foundational to our own approach to generosity. Our creator's unselfish giving is the greatest example of generosity known to mankind.

"For God so loved the world, that he gave his only begotten Son, that whosoever believeth in him should not perish, but have everlasting life." (John 3:16)

God's giving is motivated by love; a selfless, sacrificial love that knows no bounds.

"Every good gift and every perfect gift is from above, and cometh down from the Father of lights, with whom is no variableness, neither shadow of turning." (James 1:17)

His giving is characterized by constancy and perfection as emphasized in the Scripture.

"And we have known and believed the love that God hath to us. God is love; and he that dwelleth in love dwelleth in God, and God in him." (1 John 4:16)

Our giving must mirror God's in that it is motivated by love, consistent, and reflective of His nature.

Our attitude in giving is of paramount importance. As the stewards of God's blessings, we are reminded of this.

"And though I bestow all my goods to feed the poor, and though I give my body to be burned, and have not charity, it profiteth me nothing." (1 Corinthians 13:3)

Our generosity must be accompanied by love, a love that seeks the well-being of others above our own, as we are exhorted by Paul.

"Every man according as he purposeth in his heart, so let him give; not grudgingly, or of necessity: for God loveth a cheerful giver." (2 Corinthians 9:7)

Our giving must be cheerful and voluntary, born out of a heart overflowing with gratitude for God's abundant blessings. We find this sentiment reflected by God as regarding the children of Israel.

A Journey into Biblical Stewardship

"Speak unto the children of Israel, that they bring me an offering: of every man that giveth it willingly with his heart ye shall take my offering." (Exodus 25:2)

Our giving must be willing and from the heart, reflecting our genuine desire to honor God with our resources.

Finally, our approach to giving must be guided by the principles laid out in God's Word. Our instructions begin with the demonstrating our honor ro God by giving from all increase of our substance.

"Honour the Lord with thy substance, and with the firstfruits of all thine increase." (Proverbs 3:9)

Our giving must be marked by reverence and honor towards God, acknowledging Him as the source of all our blessings. This is further reinforced by Paul.

"Every man according as he purposeth in his heart, so let him give; not grudgingly, or of necessity: for God loveth a cheerful giver." (2 Corinthians 9:7)

Our giving must be voluntary and cheerful, not coerced or compelled by external factors. Yet there is importance placed of prioritizing God in our giving,

"Thou shalt not delay to offer the first of thy ripe fruits, and of thy liquors: the firstborn of thy sons shalt thou give unto me." (Exodus 22:29)

Thus, we see our giving must be marked by promptness and obedience, honoring God with the first fruits of all our increase. This also leads us to the communal aspect of giving:

"Then the disciples, every man according to his ability, determined to send relief unto the brethren which dwelt in Judaea." (Acts 11:29)

Our giving must be characterized by unity and solidarity, as we support and uplift one another in times of need.

A Journey into Biblical Stewardship

By embracing the Biblical imperative of generosity, we find that it is not merely a duty, but a privilege bestowed upon us as stewards of God's blessings. In our journey thru the principles of Biblical stewardship, may we heed the call to embrace a spirit of generosity and giving, such that those around us can see the reflection of the boundless love and abundant provision of our Heavenly Father.

A Journey into Biblical Stewardship

A Journey into Biblical Stewardship

Chapter Nine

A Godly Work Ethic

The concept of work is a cornerstone of Biblical stewardship, encompassing much more than the mere management of material resources. It is a reflection of how we conduct ourselves in every aspect of life, particularly in our work. A Biblical work ethic is fundamental to true stewardship, serving as an expression of our service to God. As stewards of the talents and opportunities God has entrusted to us, we are called to work with faithfulness, approaching our tasks with diligence, integrity, and a spirit of excellence. When we recognize that our labor is ultimately an act of worship to God, we understand that work, deeply embedded in the Biblical narrative, mirrors God's character and His design for humanity. From the very beginning of creation, God established work as a vital component of human existence, giving us the responsibility of stewardship over His creation. The Biblical work ethic is not just about laboring for survival; it encompasses a broader purpose rooted in honoring God, serving others, and fulfilling our divine calling.

The foundation of a godly work ethic is established early in the Scriptures.

> *"And the Lord God took the man, and put him into the garden of Eden to dress it and to keep it." (Genesis 2:15)*

This directive to Adam reveals that work is part of God's original plan for humanity. Work was not a consequence of the fall; rather, it was an integral aspect of the ideal human existence. God entrusted Adam with the responsibility of tending and keeping the garden, signifying that work is a noble and purposeful endeavor.

Furthermore, the cultural mandate given in emphasizes the significance of human labor in fulfilling God's purposes on earth:

A Journey into Biblical Stewardship

"And God blessed them, and God said unto them, Be fruitful, and multiply, and replenish the earth, and subdue it: and have dominion over the fish of the sea, and over the fowl of the air, and over every living thing that moveth upon the earth." (Genesis 1:28)

Work is thus an expression of our role as stewards, partnering with God in the ongoing care and development of His creation. Even the act of creation itself underscores the dignity of work:

"And God saw every thing that he had made, and, behold, it was very good." (Genesis 1:31)

God's work of creation was both deliberate and excellent, setting a divine example for us to follow. As we work, we reflect the image of our Creator, who is Himself a worker.

Work is also a means of providing for our needs and the needs of our families. The Bible highlights the importance of diligence and responsibility in labor.

"He that tilleth his land shall be satisfied with bread: but he that followeth vain persons is void of understanding." (Proverbs 12:11)

This illustrates that hard work and dedication lead to provision and satisfaction, while idleness results in lack and unfulfilled potential. The Apostle Paul reinforces this principle in his letters to the early church when he states:

"For even when we were with you, this we commanded you, that if any would not work, neither should he eat." (2 Thessalonians 3:10)

Paul's instruction underscores the expectation that every able-bodied person should contribute to their own sustenance and not rely on others when they are capable of working. This principle of self-reliance and responsibility is central to a Biblical work ethic.

A godly work ethic extends beyond self-sustenance to include serving others.

"Let him that stole steal no more: but rather let him labour, working with his hands the thing which is good, that he may have to give to him that needeth." (Ephesians 4:28)

A Journey into Biblical Stewardship

As presented here, work is not just as a means of personal provision, but also as a way to contribute to the well-being of others. By working diligently, we generate resources that can be used to support those in need, embodying the Biblical call to love and serve our neighbors. Jesus Himself modeled a servant's heart in His earthly ministry.

"For even the Son of man came not to be ministered unto, but to minister, and to give his life a ransom for many." (Mark 10:45)

Christ's example of sacrificial service provides a profound framework for understanding our work as a means of serving others. Whether through our professions, volunteer efforts, or acts of kindness, we are called to use our work to bless and uplift those around us.

Notice that the Bible calls us to pursue excellence and integrity in all our endeavors.

"And whatsoever ye do, do it heartily, as to the Lord, and not unto men; Knowing that of the Lord ye shall receive the reward of the inheritance: for ye serve the Lord Christ." (Colossians 3:23-24)

The emphasis here is that our ultimate accountability in work is to God, not merely to human supervisors or clients. For this reason, we are to approach our tasks with wholehearted dedication, striving for excellence in everything we do, remembering that integrity is another cornerstone of a Biblical work ethic.

"A false balance is abomination to the Lord: but a just weight is his delight." (Proverbs 11:1)

Honesty and fairness are essential in all our business dealings as well as our personal and professional conduct. Upholding integrity in our work reflects our commitment to God's standards and builds trust with those we serve and collaborate with.

While the Bible emphasizes the importance of hard work, it also provides wisdom on the necessity of rest and balance.

"And on the seventh day God ended his work which he had made; and he rested on the seventh day from all his work which he had made. And God blessed the seventh day, and sanctified it: because

A Journey into Biblical Stewardship

> *that in it he had rested from all his work which God created and made." (Genesis 2:2-3)*

God's rest on the seventh day sets a divine precedent for the rhythm of work and rest, with this concept of the Sabbath is further detailed in Scripture.

> *"Remember the sabbath day, to keep it holy. Six days shalt thou labour, and do all thy work: But the seventh day is the sabbath of the Lord thy God: in it thou shalt not do any work." (Exodus 20:8-10)*

This underscores the importance of setting aside time for rest, worship, and renewal. Rest is not only a physical necessity but also a spiritual discipline that acknowledges our dependence on God and His provision.

Understanding work as a divine calling transforms our perspective and approach. Our vocations are not merely secular activities but are callings from God, intended to be pursued with a sense of purpose and dedication.

> *"But as God hath distributed to every man, as the Lord hath called every one, so let him walk. And so ordain I in all churches." (1 Corinthians 7:17)*

This indicates that our vocations are not merely secular activities but are callings from God, intended to be pursued with a sense of purpose and dedication. Each individual has unique gifts and talents, which are to be utilized for God's glory and the benefit of others.

> *"Having then gifts differing according to the grace that is given to us, whether prophecy, let us prophesy according to the proportion of faith; Or ministry, let us wait on our ministering: or he that teacheth, on teaching; Or he that exhorteth, on exhortation: he that giveth, let him do it with simplicity; he that ruleth, with diligence; he that sheweth mercy, with cheerfulness." (Romans 12:6-8)*

Embracing our work as a calling encourages us to seek God's guidance in our careers and to use our talents to make a meaningful impact in the world.

A Journey into Biblical Stewardship

The journey to maintaining a godly work ethic is not without challenges. The Bible acknowledges the hardships and frustrations associated with work.

" And unto Adam he said, Because thou hast hearkened unto the voice of thy wife, and hast eaten of the tree, of which I commanded thee, saying, Thou shalt not eat of it: cursed is the ground for thy sake; in sorrow shalt thou eat of it all the days of thy life; Thorns also and thistles shall it bring forth to thee; and thou shalt eat the herb of the field; In the sweat of thy face shalt thou eat bread, till thou return unto the ground; for out of it wast thou taken: for dust thou art, and unto dust shalt thou return." (Genesis 3:17-19)

This post-fall reality reflects the toil and difficulty that often accompany our labor. Despite these challenges, Scripture provides encouragement and hope.

"And let us not be weary in well doing: for in due season we shall reap, if we faint not." (Galatians 6:9)

Perseverance in the face of adversity is a key aspect of a Biblical work ethic. Trusting in God's faithfulness, we can endure and find purpose even in the most difficult circumstances.

Ultimately, a Biblical work ethic is anchored in an eternal perspective.

"If ye then be risen with Christ, seek those things which are above, where Christ sitteth on the right hand of God. Set your affection on things above, not on things on the earth." (Colossians 3:1-2)

Recognizing that our earthly labor has eternal significance motivates us to approach our work with diligence and devotion, knowing that we are serving a higher purpose. Scripture also offers a glimpse of the eternal reward for faithful labor:

"And I heard a voice from heaven saying unto me, Write, Blessed are the dead which die in the Lord from henceforth: Yea, saith the Spirit, that they may rest from their labours; and their works do follow them." (Revelation 14:13)

A Journey into Biblical Stewardship

Our work, when done in accordance with God's will and for His glory, has lasting value and will be rewarded in eternity.

The journey to Biblical stewardship encompasses a robust and godly work ethic that is multifaceted and deeply rooted in Scripture. The journey to a godly work ethic is not just about diligence and hard work but about understanding our labor as part of our divine calling. From the creation mandate to the teachings of Jesus and the apostolic instructions, the Bible provides comprehensive guidance on the significance of work. As stewards of God's creation, we are called to work diligently, serve others, uphold integrity, balance labor with rest, and maintain an eternal perspective. When we approach our work with a Biblical perspective, we honor God, serve others, and fulfill the purpose for which we were created. Embracing these principles may transform our approach to work, while committing to a journey of faithful stewardship will have us embodying a work ethic that reflects the character of God, allowing us to honor Him, and fulfill our divine calling in every aspect of our lives.

A Journey into Biblical Stewardship

Sustainable Stewardship - A Biblical Perspective

While on this journey to Biblical stewardship, a guiding principle emerges that directs believers toward responsible care for God's creation: what society today calls sustainability. As stewards of God's creation, we are entrusted with the care and management of the earth and its resources. This responsibility is deeply rooted in Scripture, reflecting God's original mandate to humanity and His desire for us to preserve and protect His handiwork for future generations.

At the dawn of creation, God entrusted humanity with dominion over the earth, accompanied by a charge to care for and nurture His creation. Since creation there has been a divine mandate which is encapsulated as follows:

"And God blessed them, and God said unto them, Be fruitful, and multiply, and replenish the earth, and subdue it: and have dominion over the fish of the sea, and over the fowl of the air, and over every living thing that moveth upon the earth." (Genesis 1:28)

God's intention for humanity to responsibly manage the resources of the earth, ensuring their sustainability for generations to come is clearly demonstrated.

Throughout Scripture, the theme of stewardship and sustainability reverberates, underscoring the importance of caring for God's creation. David makes the following proclamation:

"The earth is the Lord's, and the fulness thereof; the world, and they that dwell therein." (Psalm 24:1)

This declaration serves as a poignant reminder that the earth and all its inhabitants belong to God, and we are merely stewards entrusted with

A Journey into Biblical Stewardship

their care. As stewards, it is our responsibility to ensure that the earth's resources are utilized wisely and sustainably, in alignment with God's purposes and principles.

Central to the concept of sustainable stewardship is the preservation and protection of God's creation. Notice why Adam and Eve were placed in Garden of Eden.

> *"And the Lord God took the man, and put him into the garden of Eden to dress it and to keep it." (Genesis 2:15)*

This charge extends beyond mere cultivation; it encompasses the nurturing and safeguarding of God's garden. As stewards, we are called to be caretakers of the earth, ensuring its health and vitality for present and future generations.

The Biblical principle of sustainability emphasizes the interconnectedness of all creation and the importance of preserving ecological balance. God gave the following instructions to the Israelites:

> *"The land shall not be sold for ever: for the land is mine, for ye are strangers and sojourners with me." (Leviticus 25:23)*

This command reflects God's ownership of the land and His desire for it to be managed with reverence and respect. Solomon gives us a reminder of this.

> *"Whoso keepeth the fig tree shall eat the fruit thereof: so he that waiteth on his master shall be honoured." (Proverbs 27:18)*

Our faithful stewardship of God's creation brings honor and blessing, both to us and to future generations.

Furthermore, sustainable stewardship encompasses not only the preservation of the earth's resources but also the protection of its inhabitants. God gave the following command:

> *"When thou shalt besiege a city a long time, in making war against it to take it, thou shalt not destroy the trees thereof by forcing an axe against them: for thou mayest eat of them, and thou shalt not cut them down (for the tree of the field is man's life) to employ them in*

A Journey into Biblical Stewardship

the siege: Only the trees which thou knowest that they be not trees for meat, thou shalt destroy and cut them down; and thou shalt build bulwarks against the city that maketh war with thee, until it be subdued." (Deuteronomy 20:19-20)

This passage illustrates God's concern for the welfare of all His creation, urging us to consider the long-term consequences of our actions and to prioritize sustainability in all our endeavors. As we journey through the teachings of Jesus Christ, we find timeless lessons on sustainable living embedded within His words and actions. We find Jesus admonishes His disciples, saying:

"Therefore I say unto you, Take no thought for your life, what ye shall eat, or what ye shall drink; nor yet for your body, what ye shall put on. Is not the life more than meat, and the body than raiment? Behold the fowls of the air: for they sow not, neither do they reap, nor gather into barns; yet your heavenly Father feedeth them. Are ye not much better than they?" (*Matthew 6:25-26*)

Jesus emphasizes the importance of trusting in God's provision and living with simplicity and contentment, rather than indulging in excessive consumption and materialism.

Moreover, Jesus' parables often convey profound truths about stewardship and sustainability. In the Parable of the Talents (read *Matthew 25:14-30*), Jesus teaches about the importance of faithful stewardship and the accountability we have for the resources entrusted to us.

"For unto every one that hath shall be given, and he shall have abundance: but from him that hath not shall be taken away even that which he hath. And cast ye the unprofitable servant into outer darkness: there shall be weeping and gnashing of teeth."
(Matthew 25:29-30)

Similarly, in the Parable of the Rich Fool (read *Luke 12:16-21*), Jesus warns against the dangers of greed and the folly of storing up treasures on earth, urging His followers to prioritize heavenly treasures and invest in the kingdom of God.

A Journey into Biblical Stewardship

"But God said unto him, Thou fool, this night thy soul shall be required of thee: then whose shall those things be, which thou hast provided? So is he that layeth up treasure for himself, and is not rich toward God." (Luke 12:20-21)

As we delve into the writings of the Apostle Paul, we find further insights into sustainable stewardship and its implications for Christian living. Paul writes the following:

"For the earnest expectation of the creature waiteth for the manifestation of the sons of God. For the creature was made subject to vanity, not willingly, but by reason of him who hath subjected the same in hope, Because the creature itself also shall be delivered from the bondage of corruption into the glorious liberty of the children of God. For we know that the whole creation groaneth and travaileth in pain together until now." (Romans 8:19-22)

Paul highlights the interconnectedness of all creation and the shared longing for redemption and restoration.

Paul admonishes believers to be good stewards of God's gifts and to use them for the benefit of others.

"Let a man so account of us, as of the ministers of Christ, and stewards of the mysteries of God. Moreover it is required in stewards, that a man be found faithful." (1 Corinthians 4:1-2)

This exhortation underscores the importance of faithful stewardship and the accountability we have for the resources entrusted to us by God.

While not often spoken of, the Biblical principle of sustainability is woven throughout Scripture, reflecting God's desire for us to responsibly care for and manage His creation. As stewards of God's earth, we are called to preserve and protect its resources for future generations, ensuring that all inhabitants can flourish and thrive. As we continue through the journey to Biblical stewardship, we discover this timeless truth, and practical wisdom, for sustainable living, rooted in a deep reverence for God and His creation. May we embrace our role as faithful stewards, cultivating a lifestyle rooted in a deep reverence for God and His creation, and cultivate a lifestyle that honors Him in all we do.

A Journey into Biblical Stewardship

Chapter Eleven

Wise Planning

Biblical stewardship encompasses the responsible management of all that God has entrusted to us, including our time, talents, and treasures. Central to effective stewardship is the principle of wise planning. Through careful and thoughtful planning, believers can honor God, make the most of their resources, and fulfill their God-given purposes.

To begin we need to see the Biblical Foundation for Wise Planning. The Bible provides clear guidance on the value and necessity of planning. God Himself is depicted as a planner, creating the universe with order and purpose. God has intentional plans for His people:

"For I know the thoughts that I think toward you, saith the Lord, thoughts of peace, and not of evil, to give you an expected end."
(Jeremiah 29:11)

Just as God plans for the welfare of His people, He calls us to plan wisely in our stewardship.

Wisdom is a recurring theme in Scripture, closely associated with planning.

"A man's heart deviseth his way: but the Lord directeth his steps."
(Proverbs 16:9)

This underscores the importance of making plans while recognizing God's ultimate sovereignty over our lives. Wise planning involves seeking God's guidance and aligning our plans with His will.

The book of Proverbs frequently uses practical examples from nature to illustrate wisdom in planning.

A Journey into Biblical Stewardship

"Go to the ant, thou sluggard; consider her ways, and be wise: Which having no guide, overseer, or ruler, Provideth her meat in the summer, and gathereth her food in the harvest." (Proverbs 6:6-8)

The ant's diligent preparation for the future serves as a model for believers, emphasizing the importance of foresight and proactive planning.

Wise planning often involves seeking counsel from others. We are reminded of this in Scripture.

"Without counsel purposes are disappointed: but in the multitude of counsellors they are established." (Proverbs 15:22)

Seeking counsel helps us avoid pitfalls and make informed decisions. This highlights the value of gaining insights and advice from trusted advisors to ensure well-rounded and effective planning.

To embrace wise planning as part of Biblical stewardship, believers can adhere to several key principles derived from Scripture.

1. **Seek God's Guidance** - The foundation of wise planning is seeking God's guidance in all our decisions. We find instructions for this in God's Word.

   "Trust in the Lord with all thine heart; and lean not unto thine own understanding. In all thy ways acknowledge him, and he shall direct thy paths." (Proverbs 3:5-6)

   By committing our plans to the Lord and seeking His wisdom, we can ensure that our steps are directed by His divine purpose.

2. **Prioritize Goals** - Setting clear and prioritized goals is essential for effective planning. Jesus Himself emphasized the importance of prioritization:

   "For which of you, intending to build a tower, sitteth not down first, and counteth the cost, whether he have sufficient to finish it? Lest haply, after he hath laid the foundation, and is not able to finish it, all that behold it begin to mock him." (Luke 14:28-30)

A Journey into Biblical Stewardship

Establishing priorities helps us allocate resources wisely and avoid overextending ourselves.

3. ***Be Diligent and Proactive*** - Diligence and proactivity are vital components of wise planning.

   "The thoughts of the diligent tend only to plenteousness; but of every one that is hasty only to want." (Proverbs 21:5)

   By being thorough and proactive in our planning, we can achieve greater success and avoid unnecessary setbacks. This verse highlights the benefits of diligent planning and the consequences of haste.

4. ***Plan for the Future*** - Wise planning involves preparing for the future and considering potential risks and uncertainties.

   "A prudent man foreseeth the evil, and hideth himself; but the simple pass on, and are punished." (Proverbs 27:12)

   Anticipating future challenges and making contingency plans help us navigate uncertainties with confidence and resilience.

5. **Balance Planning with Flexibility** - While planning is essential, it is also important to remain flexible and adaptable. We are given cautions against presumptive planning without acknowledging God's sovereignty.

   "Go to now, ye that say, To day or to morrow we will go into such a city, and continue there a year, and buy and sell, and get gain: Whereas ye know not what shall be on the morrow. For what is your life? It is even a vapour, that appeareth for a little time, and then vanisheth away. For that ye ought to say, If the Lord will, we shall live, and do this, or that." (James 4:13-15)

Balancing planning with a humble recognition of God's control allows us to adapt when circumstances change.

A Journey into Biblical Stewardship

Implementing wise planning requires practical steps that align with Biblical principles. Here are some actionable steps to guide believers in their planning efforts.

1. **Establish a Vision and Mission** - A clear vision and mission provide direction and purpose for our planning.

   "Where there is no vision, the people perish: but he that keepeth the law, happy is he." (Proverbs 29:18)

   By defining our vision and mission, we can align our plans with God's purposes and stay focused on our goals.

2. **Set SMART Goals** - Setting SMART (Specific, Measurable, Achievable, Relevant, Time-bound) goals helps us create actionable and realistic plans. Believers are encouraged to press toward their goals:

   "Brethren, I count not myself to have apprehended: but this one thing I do, forgetting those things which are behind, and reaching forth unto those things which are before, I press toward the mark for the prize of the high calling of God in Christ Jesus." (Philippians 3:13-14)

   SMART goals provide a clear roadmap for achieving our objectives.

3. **Create a Detailed Plan** - A detailed plan outlines the steps needed to achieve our goals. Jesus illustrates the importance of planning.

   "For which of you, intending to build a tower, sitteth not down first, and counteth the cost, whether he have sufficient to finish it?" (Luke 14:28-30)

   A well-thought-out plan considers resources, timelines, and potential obstacles, ensuring that we are prepared for each phase of our journey.

A Journey into Biblical Stewardship

4. **Monitor Progress and Adjust** - Regularly monitoring progress and making necessary adjustments are crucial for effective planning.

   "Prepare thy work without, and make it fit for thyself in the field; and afterwards build thine house." (Proverbs 24:27)

   By tracking our progress and being willing to adjust our plans, we can stay on course and adapt to changing circumstances.

5. **Trust in God's Provision** - Throughout the planning process, it is essential to trust in God's provision and guidance. We have the assurance of God that:

   "But my God shall supply all your need according to his riches in glory by Christ Jesus." (Philippians 4:19)

   Trusting in God's provision helps us remain confident and faithful, knowing that He will provide for our needs as we pursue His purposes.

Wise planning yields numerous benefits, enhancing our ability to steward God's resources effectively and fulfill His purposes.

1. **Greater Efficiency and Productivity** - Wise planning increases efficiency and productivity by providing a clear roadmap for achieving our goals.

   "Commit thy works unto the Lord, and thy thoughts shall be established." (Proverbs 16:3)

   By planning wisely, we can make the most of our time and resources, accomplishing more for God's kingdom.

2. **Enhanced Decision-Making** - Effective planning improves decision-making by providing a framework for evaluating options and anticipating outcomes.

   "There are many devices in a man's heart; nevertheless the counsel of the Lord, that shall stand." (Proverbs 19:21)

A Journey into Biblical Stewardship

With a well-constructed plan, we can make informed decisions that align with God's will.

3. **Reduced Stress and Anxiety** - Having a plan in place reduces stress and anxiety by providing clarity and direction. Jesus encourages us to trust in God's provision.

   "Take therefore no thought for the morrow: for the morrow shall take thought for the things of itself. Sufficient unto the day is the evil thereof." (Matthew 6:34)

   A clear plan helps us navigate challenges with confidence and peace, knowing that God is in control.

4. **Increased Financial Stability** - Wise financial planning promotes stability and security, enabling us to manage resources effectively and avoid unnecessary debt.

   "There is treasure to be desired and oil in the dwelling of the wise; but a foolish man spendeth it up." (Proverbs 21:20)

   By planning our finances wisely, we can build a solid foundation for the future and support God's work more effectively.

5. Greater Impact for God's Kingdom - Ultimately, wise planning enhances our ability to impact God's kingdom. We are exhorted as believers to live wisely.

   "See then that ye walk circumspectly, not as fools, but as wise, Redeeming the time, because the days are evil. Wherefore be ye not unwise, but understanding what the will of the Lord is." (Ephesians 5:15-17)

   By planning our time, talents, and treasures effectively, we can maximize our impact and contribute to God's redemptive purposes.

Our journey to Biblical stewardship must be marked by wise planning which is guided by the principles and wisdom of Scripture. By seeking God's guidance, prioritizing goals, being diligent and

A Journey into Biblical Stewardship

proactive, planning for the future, and balancing planning with flexibility, believers can steward their resources effectively and fulfill their God-given purposes. The benefits of wise planning are numerous, including greater efficiency, enhanced decision-making, reduced stress, increased financial stability, and a greater impact for God's kingdom. As we commit our plans to the Lord and trust in His provision, we can navigate the journey of stewardship with confidence and faithfulness, bringing glory to God in all that we do.

A Journey into Biblical Stewardship

A Journey into Biblical Stewardship

Debt Avoidance

While the journey to Biblical stewardship is a path marked by various aspects of stewardship such as faithfulness, integrity, and obedience to God's Word, the avoidance of debt is a critical principle that aligns with the teachings of Scripture. Debt can be a significant hindrance to effective stewardship. It binds individuals and families, limiting their ability to give generously, save for the future, and live freely according to God's principles. The Bible provides clear guidance on managing finances and avoiding debt, which is an essential part of faithful stewardship. The Biblical teachings on debt avoidance offer practical advice on how to manage resources wisely and maintain financial freedom, providing practical guidance for those who seek to honor God through wise financial management.

The Bible offers clear guidance on the dangers and implications of debt. Debt can place individuals in a position of bondage and compromise their ability to fulfill God's purposes for their lives.

"The rich ruleth over the poor, and the borrower is servant to the lender." (Proverbs 22:7)

Highlighting the inherent power imbalance created by debt, this verse aims at revealing the fact that the borrower becomes subservient to the lender. God's desire for His people is freedom and not bondage. Consider Paul's admonition to believers:

"Owe no man any thing, but to love one another: for he that loveth another hath fulfilled the law". (Romans 13:8)

This instruction underscores the importance of financial freedom, enabling believers to focus on loving and serving others rather than being encumbered by financial obligations.

A Journey into Biblical Stewardship

Debt can have far-reaching consequences, affecting not only the individual's financial well-being but also their spiritual health and relationships. Solomon gives us warnings concerning this.

"Be not thou one of them that strike hands, or of them that are sureties for debts. If thou hast nothing to pay, why should he take away thy bed from under thee?" (Proverbs 22:26-27)

This passage cautions against the pitfalls of co-signing or guaranteeing another person's debt, which can lead to severe financial repercussions. Scripture goes deeper, indicating that the weight of debt can also hinder one's ability to give generously and support the work of God's kingdom. We find that God challenges His people to bring their tithes into the storehouse, promising to pour out blessings in return:

"Bring ye all the tithes into the storehouse, that there may be meat in mine house, and prove me now herewith, saith the Lord of hosts, if I will not open you the windows of heaven, and pour you out a blessing, that there shall not be room enough to receive it." (Malachi 3:10)

When burdened by debt, believers may find it difficult to fulfill this command, thereby missing out on God's promised blessings.

To avoid the pitfalls of debt, believers can adhere to several Biblical principles that promote wise financial management and stewardship such as:

1. **Live Within Your Means**. Living within one's means is a foundational principle for avoiding debt.

   "There is treasure to be desired and oil in the dwelling of the wise; but a foolish man spendeth it up." (Proverbs 21:20)

   This verse contrasts the wisdom of saving and conserving resources with the folly of reckless spending. By living within their means, believers can avoid accumulating debt and ensure that they have sufficient resources for future needs.

A Journey into Biblical Stewardship

2. **Plan and Budget.** Effective planning and budgeting are essential for maintaining financial stability and avoiding debt.

   "Through wisdom is an house builded; and by understanding it is established: And by knowledge shall the chambers be filled with all precious and pleasant riches." (Proverbs 24:3-4)

   We see here that the This passage emphasizes the importance of wisdom and understanding in managing household affairs, which includes prudent financial planning. Creating a budget allows believers to allocate their resources wisely, prioritize their spending, and avoid unnecessary debt.

3. **Save and Invest.** Saving and investing are crucial components of financial stewardship. Consider how Solomon extols the virtues of the ant, a creature known for its industriousness and foresight.

   "Go to the ant, thou sluggard; consider her ways, and be wise: Which having no guide, overseer, or ruler, Provideth her meat in the summer, and gathereth her food in the harvest." (Proverbs 6:6-8)

   By saving and investing, believers can prepare for future needs and emergencies, reducing their reliance on debt.

4. **Avoid Impulsive Purchases.** Impulsive purchases can lead to unnecessary debt and financial strain.

   "The thoughts of the diligent tend only to plenteousness; but of every one that is hasty only to want." (Proverbs 21:5)

   This verse highlights the value of diligent planning and the dangers of hasty decisions. By exercising self-control and avoiding impulsive purchases, believers can maintain financial discipline and avoid debt.

A Journey into Biblical Stewardship

5. **Seek Wise Counsel**. Seeking wise counsel is a Biblical principle that can help believers make informed financial decisions and avoid debt.

   "Without counsel purposes are disappointed: but in the multitude of counsellors they are established." (Proverbs 15:22)

   By consulting with knowledgeable and trustworthy advisors, believers can gain valuable insights and guidance for managing their finances effectively.

For those who are already in debt, the Bible offers hope and practical steps for overcoming financial burdens and achieving freedom.

1. **Acknowledge and Repent**. The first step in overcoming debt is to acknowledge the problem and repent of any financial mismanagement.

   "If we confess our sins, he is faithful and just to forgive us our sins, and to cleanse us from all unrighteousness." (1 John 1:9)

   We are assured that by confessing and seeking God's forgiveness, believers can begin the journey to financial restoration with a renewed commitment to Biblical principles.

2. **Create a Repayment Plan** Developing a repayment plan is essential for systematically reducing and eventually eliminating debt.

   "Be thou diligent to know the state of thy flocks, and look well to thy herds." (Proverbs 27:23)

   Notice how this underscores the importance of diligently managing one's resources. By creating a detailed repayment plan, believers can prioritize their debts, allocate funds appropriately, and track their progress.

A Journey into Biblical Stewardship

3. **Exercise Discipline and Patience**   Paying off debt requires discipline and patience.

    "Now no chastening for the present seemeth to be joyous, but grievous: nevertheless afterward it yieldeth the peaceable fruit of righteousness unto them which are exercised thereby." (Hebrews 12:11)

    Although the process of repaying debt may be challenging, it ultimately leads to the peace and freedom that comes from financial stability.

4. **Trust in God's Provision**   Throughout the journey of debt repayment, believers must trust in God's provision and faithfulness.

    "But my God shall supply all your need according to his riches in glory by Christ Jesus." (Philippians 4:19)

    By relying on God's promises and seeking His guidance, believers can find the strength and resources needed to overcome debt.

Following these practical steps for overcoming financial burdens will aide in achieving freedom, following them will bring hope as the move toward debt-free living comes closer.

Living debt-free brings numerous blessings, enabling believers to experience greater peace, freedom, and opportunities for generosity.

1. **Financial Freedom**   Debt-free living provides financial freedom, allowing believers to make decisions without the constraints of financial obligations. Solomon warns against the consequences of debt.

    "Be not thou one of them that strike hands, or of them that are sureties for debts. If thou hast nothing to pay, why should he take away thy bed from under thee?"   (Proverbs 22:26-27)

A Journey into Biblical Stewardship

Financial freedom enables believers to live with less stress and greater security.

2. **Increased Generosity** Without the burden of debt, believers are better positioned to give generously and support God's work. Paul encourages cheerful giving.

> *"Every man according as he purposeth in his heart, so let him give; not grudgingly, or of necessity: for God loveth a cheerful giver." (2 Corinthians 9:7)*

Debt-free living allows believers to respond to the needs of others with open hearts and hands.

3. **Greater Stewardship Opportunities** Debt-free living enhances believers' ability to steward their resources effectively, investing in opportunities that align with God's purposes. Jesus teaches,

> *"He that is faithful in that which is least is faithful also in much: and he that is unjust in the least is unjust also in much." (Luke 16:10)*

By managing their finances wisely and avoiding debt, believers can be entrusted with greater responsibilities and blessings.

4. **Enhanced Spiritual Growth** Living debt-free contributes to spiritual growth by fostering trust in God's provision and cultivating a heart of contentment. Paul shares his secret of contentment.

> *"Not that I speak in respect of want: for I have learned, in whatsoever state I am, therewith to be content. I know both how to be abased, and I know how to abound: every where and in all things I am instructed both to be full and to be hungry, both to abound and to suffer need. I can do all things through Christ which strengtheneth me." (Philippians 4:11-13)*

Financial freedom allows believers to focus more on their relationship with God and less on material concerns.

A Journey into Biblical Stewardship

The journey to Biblical stewardship is marked by the intentional avoidance of debt, guided by the principles and wisdom of Scripture. By living within their means, planning and budgeting, saving and investing, avoiding impulsive purchases, and seeking wise counsel, believers can honor God with their finances and experience the blessings of debt-free living. For those already in debt, acknowledging the problem, creating a repayment plan, exercising discipline and patience, and trusting in God's provision can lead to financial restoration and freedom. Ultimately, debt-free living enhances believers' ability to serve God, support His work, and grow spiritually. As we embrace the principles of Biblical stewardship, let us echo the words of the psalmist, declaring:

"The earth is the Lord's, and the fulness thereof; the world, and they that dwell therein." (Psalms 24:1)

A Journey into Biblical Stewardship

A Journey into Biblical Stewardship

Stewardship with an Eternal Perspective

Biblical stewardship is more than a practical application of managing resources wisely; it is fundamentally rooted in an eternal perspective that transcends the temporal pursuits of this world. Unlike the temporal pursuits of this world, which often focus on immediate gratification and personal gain, this eternal viewpoint shapes our values, decisions, and actions, aligning them with God's will and purposes. By understanding and embracing an eternal perspective, we become better stewards of the gifts God has entrusted to us, recognizing that our ultimate goal is to honor Him and advance His kingdom.

The Bible frequently contrasts the fleeting nature of earthly possessions with the enduring value of heavenly treasures. Jesus' teachings in the Sermon on the Mount highlight this distinction:

"Lay not up for yourselves treasures upon earth, where moth and rust doth corrupt, and where thieves break through and steal: But lay up for yourselves treasures in heaven, where neither moth nor rust doth corrupt, and where thieves do not break through nor steal: For where your treasure is, there will your heart be also."
(Matthew 6:19-21)

Jesus takes time to underscore the importance of prioritizing eternal investments over temporal gains, as earthly treasures are vulnerable to decay and theft.

Paul reinforces this call to focus on the eternal in his letter to the Corinthians:

"While we look not at the things which are seen, but at the things which are not seen: for the things which are seen are temporal; but the things which are not seen are eternal." (2 Corinthians 4:18)

A Journey into Biblical Stewardship

This perspective helps us to shift our focus from the visible and temporary to the invisible and everlasting, guiding our stewardship practices towards what truly matters in God's eternal plan.

Stewardship that is grounded in an eternal perspective aligns with God's purposes and reflects His values.

"Set your affection on things above, not on things on the earth." (Colossians 3:2)

By focusing on heavenly values, our stewardship efforts become an expression of our commitment to God's kingdom and His eternal purposes. The parable of the talents (read **Matthew 25:14-30**) further illustrates the connection between faithful stewardship and eternal rewards. Notice the words of the master as he commends the faithful servants:

"Well done, thou good and faithful servant: thou hast been faithful over a few things, I will make thee ruler over many things: enter thou into the joy of thy lord." (Matthew 25:21)

Notice how this parable teaches that our faithfulness in managing God's resources on earth will be rewarded in eternity, emphasizing the long-term significance of our stewardship.

Ultimately, our stewardship should aim to glorify God, reflecting His character and advancing His kingdom.

"Whether therefore ye eat, or drink, or whatsoever ye do, do all to the glory of God." (1 Corinthians 10:31)

By living for God's glory, we demonstrate an eternal perspective that transcends temporal pursuits and aligns our actions with God's eternal plan. Investing in our spiritual growth is a crucial aspect of stewardship with an eternal perspective. Peter encourages us in this manner:

"grow in grace, and in the knowledge of our Lord and Saviour Jesus Christ." (2 Peter 3:18)

By prioritizing our relationship with God and seeking to grow in our faith, we ensure that our lives are grounded in eternal values. Thus,

A Journey into Biblical Stewardship

both generosity and service are tangible expressions of eternal stewardship.

"But to do good and to communicate forget not: for with such sacrifices God is well pleased." (Hebrews 13:16)

By sharing our resources and serving others, we invest in God's kingdom and reflect His love and compassion.

Wisely managing our resources is another important aspect of eternal stewardship.

"Honour the Lord with thy substance, and with the firstfruits of all thine increase: So shall thy barns be filled with plenty, and thy presses shall burst out with new wine." (Proverbs 3:9-10)

By honoring God with our possessions and using them to advance His purposes, we demonstrate our commitment to eternal values.

Building and nurturing relationships with eternal significance is a vital component of stewardship.

"Let nothing be done through strife or vainglory; but in lowliness of mind let each esteem other better than themselves. Look not every man on his own things, but every man also on the things of others." (Philippians 2:3-4)

By valuing and investing in others, we reflect the eternal love of Christ and contribute to the growth of His kingdom.

Having an eternal perspective will be reflected in our everyday life, including our work and career, financial decisions, family and relationships, witnessing to the world, and leaving a legacy. This in turn provides us both hope and assurance. Notice how we are impacted:

1. **Work and Career** - Viewing our work and career through an eternal lens transforms how we approach our daily tasks.

   "And whatsoever ye do, do it heartily, as to the Lord, and not unto men; Knowing that of the Lord ye shall receive the reward of the inheritance: for ye serve the Lord Christ." (Colossians 3:23-24)

A Journey into Biblical Stewardship

By seeing our work as service to God, we can find purpose and fulfillment in our professional lives, knowing that our efforts contribute to His eternal plan.

2. **Financial Decisions** - Financial decisions are a significant aspect of stewardship that benefits from an eternal perspective, with warnings against placing our hope in wealth, and encouragement for us to be generous found throughout scripture.

   "Charge them that are rich in this world, that they be not highminded, nor trust in uncertain riches, but in the living God, who giveth us richly all things to enjoy; That they do good, that they be rich in good works, ready to distribute, willing to communicate; Laying up in store for themselves a good foundation against the time to come, that they may lay hold on eternal life." (1 Timothy 6:17-19)

   By making financial choices that honor God and support His work, we align our resources with eternal priorities.

3. **Family and Relationships** - Our relationships with family and friends are also enriched by an eternal perspective.

   "See then that ye walk circumspectly, not as fools, but as wise, Redeeming the time, because the days are evil." (Ephesians 5:15-16)

   By investing time and energy into our relationships, we build connections that have lasting significance and reflect the love and grace of God.

4. **Witnessing to the World** - Living with an eternal perspective serves as a powerful witness to the world as we are called to be the light to the world.

   "Ye are the light of the world. A city that is set on an hill cannot be hid. Neither do men light a candle, and put it under a bushel, but on a candlestick; and it giveth light unto all that are in the house. Let your light so shine before men, that they may see

A Journey into Biblical Stewardship

your good works, and glorify your Father which is in heaven."
(Matthew 5:14-16)

By embodying eternal values in our stewardship, we draw others to Christ and glorify God.

5. **Leaving a Legacy** - An eternal perspective helps us to leave a lasting legacy that honors God.

   "A good man leaveth an inheritance to his children's children: and the wealth of the sinner is laid up for the just."
   (Proverbs 13:22)

   By investing in the spiritual, relational, and material well-being of future generations, we ensure that our stewardship has a lasting impact that extends beyond our lifetime.

6. **Hope and Assurance** - Grounding our stewardship in an eternal perspective provides us with hope and assurance.

   "For I reckon that the sufferings of this present time are not worthy to be compared with the glory which shall be revealed in us." (Romans 8:18)

   By focusing on the eternal glory that awaits us, we can persevere through challenges and remain faithful stewards, knowing that our efforts will be rewarded in eternity.

Embracing an eternal perspective is essential for Biblical stewardship. By focusing on the lasting values of God's kingdom rather than the fleeting pursuits of this world, we align our actions with His eternal purposes. The Bible provides clear guidance on how to ground our stewardship in an eternal perspective, encouraging us to prioritize spiritual growth, generosity, wise resource management, and meaningful relationships. As we journey towards Biblical stewardship, let us continually seek to view our lives through the lens of eternity, recognizing that our ultimate goal is to glorify God and advance His kingdom.

A Journey into Biblical Stewardship

"Wherefore seeing we also are compassed about with so great a cloud of witnesses, let us lay aside every weight, and the sin which doth so easily beset us, and let us run with patience the race that is set before us, Looking unto Jesus the author and finisher of our faith; who for the joy that was set before him endured the cross, despising the shame, and is set down at the right hand of the throne of God." (Hebrews 12:1-2)

By keeping our eyes fixed on Jesus and His eternal purposes, we can faithfully steward the gifts He has entrusted to us, making a lasting impact for His glory.

A Journey into Biblical Stewardship

Chapter Fourteen

Embracing the Call to Biblical Stewardship

The principles of Biblical stewardship we have shared here present a counter-cultural paradigm, calling us to a higher purpose while living in a world which is driven by relentless consumption and materialism. These principles are not merely about managing resources; rather they are about aligning our hearts, minds, and actions with God's divine will. Knowing what we would be facing, Jesus prayed to the Father for each of us while we live in this world:

"I pray not that thou shouldest take them out of the world, but that thou shouldest keep them from the evil. They are not of the world, even as I am not of the world. Sanctify them through thy truth: thy word is truth." (John 17:15-17)

Having traversed the rich landscape of Scripture to uncover timeless truths that shape our understanding of what it means to be faithful stewards of God's creation, let us answer the call to a life of Biblical Stewardship. The life of Biblical Stewardship is a holistic, all-encompassing way of life that reflects our relationship with God, His creation, and each other. Biblical stewardship is a sacred calling, one that demands our full attention, devotion, and commitment. The principles are not just abstract concepts; they are divine mandates that call us to a higher standard of living, one that reflects God's sovereignty, grace, and purpose.

Remember, the foundation of our journey is the recognition of God's ownership over all things. As the Psalmist declares:

"The earth is the Lord's, and the fulness thereof; the world, and they that dwell therein." (Psalm 24:1)

A Journey into Biblical Stewardship

This profound truth anchors our understanding of stewardship, reminding us that everything we have, and everything we are, belongs to God. This foundational principle compels us to live with a sense of reverence and responsibility, acknowledging that we are merely caretakers of the abundant blessings God has entrusted to us.

In recognizing God as the owner, we find walking in integrity is not only central to our Christian faith but a reflection of our commitment to honor God in every aspect of our lives. Integrity calls for honesty, responsibility, and steadfastness, all of which guide us in our relationships and stewardship.

"The integrity of the upright shall guide them: but the perverseness of transgressors shall destroy them."(Proverbs 11:3)

May we strive to walk uprightly, knowing that living with integrity brings both spiritual and practical rewards, and ultimately glorifies God in all we do.

Biblical Stewardship is far more than a financial strategy or an environmental ethic; it is a holistic way of life. It encompasses every aspect of our existence, from our finances and possessions to our time, talents, and relationships. It calls us to live with integrity, purpose, and intentionality, seeking to honor God in all that we do. One of the most compelling aspects of Biblical stewardship is the principle of accountability. Paul reminds us of the simple truth:

"So then every one of us shall give account of himself to God." (Romans 14:12)

This sobering truth challenges us to manage God's resources with diligence and integrity, knowing that one day we will stand before Him to give an account of our stewardship. It is a call to live with a sense of urgency and responsibility, recognizing that our actions have eternal implications.

Faithfulness is another cornerstone of Biblical stewardship. In the parable of the talents, Jesus commends the faithful servant, saying**,**

"Well done, thou good and faithful servant: thou hast been faithful over a few things, I will make thee ruler over many things: enter thou into the joy of thy lord." (Matthew 25:21)

A Journey into Biblical Stewardship

Jesus teaches us that faithfulness in small matters leads to greater opportunities and blessings. It encourages us to use our God-given resources wisely and productively, investing in His kingdom purposes with a spirit of devotion and commitment.

In a world that constantly urges us to acquire more, the principle of contentment stands as a counter-cultural witness. Paul writes,

"Not that I speak in respect of want: for I have learned, in whatsoever state I am, therewith to be content." (Philippians 4:11)

We find contentment is a rare virtue in today's society, yet it is essential for true stewardship. It allows us to find satisfaction in God's provision, freeing us from the endless pursuit of possessions and positions.

Compassion is at the heart of Biblical stewardship. The wise king Solomon observes:

"He that hath pity upon the poor lendeth unto the Lord; and that which he hath given will he pay him again." (Proverbs 19:17)

Acts of compassion and generosity reflect God's love and grace to those in need. As we care for the marginalized and vulnerable, we embody the heart of Christ and fulfill our stewardship responsibilities.

Generosity flows naturally from a heart transformed by God's grace. Jesus teaches us:

"Give, and it shall be given unto you; good measure, pressed down, and shaken together, and running over, shall men give into your bosom. For with the same measure that ye mete withal it shall be measured to you again" (Luke 6:38)

Generosity is a reflection of God's abundant love and provision. It frees us from the grip of materialism and selfishness, enabling us to bless others and advance God's kingdom through acts of kindness and charity.

The principle of work ethic is foundational to Biblical stewardship. The Bible affirms:

"Whatsoever thy hand findeth to do, do it with thy might; for there is no work, nor device, nor knowledge, nor wisdom, in the grave, whither thou goest." (Ecclesiastes 9:10)

A Journey into Biblical Stewardship

Work is not merely a means to an end; it is a sacred calling that allows us to glorify God and serve others.

> *"And whatsoever ye do in word or deed, do all in the name of the Lord Jesus, giving thanks to God and the Father by him." (Colossians 3:17)*

By working diligently and with excellence, we fulfill our stewardship responsibilities and contribute to the flourishing of God's creation.

Sustainability through stewardship is a divine calling woven throughout Scripture, urging us to care for God's creation with wisdom and reverence. As we reflect on the teachings of Christ and the Bible, we are reminded of our responsibility to preserve the earth's resources for future generations, ensuring all life can thrive under God's provision. Let us embrace this calling as faithful stewards, always remembering:

> *"Moreover it is required in stewards, that a man be found faithful." (1 Corinthians 4:2)*

May our actions honor God and reflect His love for all creation.

Planning and foresight are integral components of faithful stewardship. The book of Proverbs teaches us:

> *"The thoughts of the diligent tend only to plenteousness; but of every one that is hasty only to want" (Proverbs 21:5)*

By seeking God's wisdom and guidance in our financial decisions, we can navigate life's uncertainties with confidence and clarity, ensuring that our plans align with His purposes.

Avoiding debt and practicing financial prudence are crucial aspects of wise stewardship. The Scriptures cautions us

> *"The rich ruleth over the poor, and the borrower is servant to the lender." (Proverbs 22:7)*

By living within our means and managing our resources wisely, we experience greater freedom and flexibility in our stewardship, enabling us to respond to God's leading with open hands and hearts.

A Journey into Biblical Stewardship

Finally, Biblical stewardship is grounded in an eternal perspective. The apostle Paul reminds us:

"For our conversation is in heaven; from whence also we look for the Saviour, the Lord Jesus Christ." (Philippians 3:20)

This eternal perspective helps us to focus on what truly matters, investing our resources in ways that have lasting significance for God's kingdom.

As we journey into Biblical stewardship, let us remember that we are not owners but stewards, not masters but servants. We are entrusted with the privilege of managing God's resources for His glory and the flourishing of His creation. May this truth inspire us to live with humility, wisdom, and joy, embracing the call to stewardship with a renewed sense of purpose and gratitude.

While we live in a world often darkened by greed, selfishness, and materialism, may we shine as beacons of light, demonstrating the beauty and richness of a life lived in faithful stewardship. As we honor God with every resource He has entrusted to our care, may our lives bring glory to His name and advance His kingdom purposes on earth. Let us go forth with open hearts and eager minds, ready to discover the boundless grace and mercy of our Heavenly Father. May we be transformed by the renewing of our minds, surrendering our wills to His, and embracing the call to stewardship with joy and gratitude. Together, let us embark on this journey, seeking to glorify God and bless others as we faithfully steward His abundant blessings.

A Journey into Biblical Stewardship

www.ingramcontent.com/pod-product-compliance
Lightning Source LLC
Chambersburg PA
CBHW070201230526
45471CB00002B/762